Son Risings

Discovering & Caring for the Real You

By

Don Mingo

Kevin & Dollie,

Wow! What a great new
friendship. Thanks for the weekend.

Don & Kathy

2 Cor 12: 8-10
Ps 40 1:3
2 Cor 1:4

Mingo Publishing Group LLC, Big Bend, Wisconsin.

Cover Photo by Eric Didier

Son Risings – Discovering and Caring for the Real You – 1st Edition

ISBN 9780692926048

Table of Contents

-1-
Lon

***"That you may prosper in all things and be in health,
just as your soul prospers."*[1]**

Standing off to the left during a Christmas Eve program Lon exclaimed, "Don! How long has it been my friend? At least twenty years I bet!" Forlorn, tired looking, and slumped forward just a bit, I thought, "Wow! You have not aged very well." Offering a customary response, "How have you been," decided the fate of my Christmas Eve service. As tears welled up in his eyes, I knew, "You won't make this Christmas Eve service."

Lon, a lay leader in his church, elected council member of his town, a business owner, and man of respectable influence in his community, stood slumped and stooped before me. In brokenness, he opened the dams of his unhappiness. An unhappiness witnessed in scores of pastors, missionaries, leaders, and churchgoers. He was clearly unwell; in an uncared-for state. It showed on his face. It resounded in his voice. His tone and inflection communicated from a once lively spirit, a sullen dark demeanor. A rather dark negative combative caustic attitude sullied the mood. Ho, Ho, Ho, Merry Christmas! Nope. Not here. Not tonight. At every level of Lon's existence, he was as he put it, "done."

In construction, at age fifty, his fortitude for the profession waned in every aspect. Who might blame him? In cold winters, what fifty-year-old wanted a job of high physicality in January? Sitting at the coffee bar in the front lobby of the church, Lon's emotions flooded our table. Emotions not prepared for nor desired on a Christmas Eve. Escaping Lon's unhappy grouchy demeanor became an immediate priority. Who needs this at Christmas? My slight leaning towards compassion changed the entire evening. Wondering if perhaps it was that time of the year; holidays, Lon's disposition indicated something else. Something deeper. A soul wrenching discontent. Something personally witnessed before with many church goers.

Thirty minutes into our conversation his eyes a tear rolled down his cheek. Imagine, a grown man crying to a guy he hadn't seen in over ten years surrounded by hundreds of people. Trying to contain his emotions, he whimpered, "Don, it's like my soul has died." His descriptive expression clasped my attention. "My soul has died," an expression heard often in Africa, but rarely in an American church context.

During the next two-hours, and another missed Christmas Eve Service, no less than a dozen times, Lon used the phrase, "My soul." His vivid descriptions painted a weary bleak soul-landscape of a once vibrant man trying to hold on. "My soul is tired. My soul is weary. It's like my soul is dead or sick." Lon's staggering disappointments on many fronts of life presented a stark contrast to the man of years gone by. His disappointment with life matched his disappointment with the church he belonged to for over thirty years. This list went on and on and on. This once vibrant man stood as a shadow of his former self. Bible teacher, leader, musician, business owner, husband, and father now fell far short of any personal expectation for success in life, career, or soul.

As Lon verbally pondered his discontented predicament, he brightened, "You know, it sort of reminds me of a Wildland fire last year." Looking for some affirmation, in the crushing noise of hundreds of people in the lobby, I offered an obliging mentally fatigued nod as the next Christmas service began. Breaking eye contact, my sweet wife emerged from the previous service smiling and making her way towards refreshments and people. This sort of thing happens quite often. She's used to it.

Lon continued, "Yes, last year I was on a job. It was a very rural area. We were building a nice vacation home for a very wealthy gentleman. While working inside we smelled smoke. Within an hour the woods were filled with smoke. We had to leave. Wildland fires were approaching our way. So, we jumped in our vehicles and tried to make our way out to the main road. It was tough because the smoke and haze was so very thick. The dirt roads we traveled to get to our jobs were almost unrecognizable because of the smoke. And, you know, that is how I . . . I, guess, I feel. Like my soul is in a kind of smoke. Like everything is hazy. Lon reached a crescendo of self-discovery blurting out, "Yes, it's like my soul is in a haze. That's it. That's where

I am. Like I don't know where I am going or what the purpose of it all is."

"My soul is in a haze." Such an unusual phrase. Isn't it? Lon's closing words hurled my mind and imagination back twenty-five years to Africa. To a special place behind my home in Ladysmith, South Africa. A place where a personal soul-epiphany occurred many years earlier. An experience that began redirecting a new journey in my soul.

-2-
Haze

"Not all those who wander are lost."
J.R.R. Tolkien, The Fellowship of the Ring

Often, especially during the winter season, those many years ago in South Africa, I availed myself the pleasure of climbing a rocky boulder strewn hill behind my home. In the rugged terrain of Northern Natal, scenery took one's breath away, never to tire of South Africa's beauty. With Bruno and Chocolate, my two lab dogs, the early hours just before sunrise awaited. As the day prepared it's beginning, a reserved spot on that small bluff always produced anticipation. The brilliancy of an early morning's arrival captured one's person witnessing the sun's grand entrance into the new day.

In that shapeless darkness just before the sunrise, fowls began their choral announcements as a celestial king approached. Hoopoes, Orioles, Weavers, Sparrows, and other feathered friends joined together in those early hours forming one grand heavenly choir. Together their voices announced the day's advance into the night's retreat. In the distance, sounds from creatures tuned their presence into one grand chorale celebrating an approaching honored guest. Simply magnificent!

Quiet strangers too bustled in the wind. These gentle giants, hiding their identities amidst blusters and breezes of the conductor's baton, announced the coming. Mere silhouettes cast themselves against a horizon's curtain. Sounding adulating joy among their leaves and branches as the wind raked them about added to the percussions. Gathered grandly, the choreographed rhythms chimed awaiting anticipation.

In the crisp, cool air, a hot cup of coffee tasted never better. Quiet streets, dark homes clumped together, and many open patches of land garnished by patches of fog layered the country side. Multitudes of hills covered with rocks surrounded by mountains provided backdrops for endless kaleidoscopes of wonder as the light began to peer through. Thus, were those many marvelous early mornings spent in the mountains of Natal in South Africa many years ago.

One morning was different from all others. In the darkness before sunrise, the often-anticipated arrival detracted from its normal grand entrance. On this day, smoke hung at the horizon's edge resulting from hundreds of brush fires burning the entire night in the surrounding farmlands. Ignited by a lightning strike in a nearby farmer's field, flames engulfed the countryside. Thousands of acres burned throughout the night.

Waiting for the Sun's brilliant entrance that morning, noticed a rather hindered crippled celebrity unable to make its normal daily entry. The sun, on this day struggled to make its grand entrance. It appeared at first as just a small slice of red faintly glowing in the distance staggering to perform as in other days. A small splinter of light developing into one small seemly ineffective disappointing glow.

The dreary country side bowed choked with the haze of a hundred fires. Shadows and darkness seemed to rule the day. The rays of new beginnings failed to make their principal showing as the early morning choir failed to arrive. No birds, no beam of light, no anticipation; nothing but dark choking smoke covered the land. Stinging burning eyes and a coarse sore throat from inhaling foul, polluted air force a disappointing retreat.

Dispirited by hazy unfamiliar surroundings, I gestured to Bruno and Chocolate as we started down the hill. What a waste of time. Or was it? Stopping in the middle of the path thoughts began pouring in from new directions. A slow about-face, another gesture, and a climb back up the bluff repurposed the morning. Expecting the normal sunrise's brilliance to introduce the day, startling thoughts changed direction flowing from another source beyond my disappointment.

How many times do expectations fail to meet experience? How many people experience life obscured by hazy uncertainties? In the African community of which I lived for so many years, struggling suffering people described their lives much liked that day.

Day after day of crowded busyness, disappointment, personal loss, and failure to arrive at hope's path dampen lives in hazy entities which vie for many souls. Expectation's sun risings occur clouded by a haze of dangers, worries, and cares of this world. Shrouded souls choke on the clutters in life. Many hope their lives will always resemble those many beautiful clear crisp mornings visited regularly by brilliant uncluttered sun risings. Sun risings that begin a new day afresh. Those kinds of mornings give hope in an often too hopeless world. Our solar system's celestial body often awakens many applauding its entrance into their lives. But, what happens when life's sun risings seem to appear not?

During that first hour that morning so many years ago, behind my home in South Africa, as the sun struggled, darkness appeared to win a rare victory shrouding every tree, hill, rock, and valley. Darkness and haze battling for control of the day appeared to win victory. Choking smoke blocked the sun's anticipated beauty. The sun appeared to fail in its arrival. Yet, while not seen, the sun that morning changed not. Consistent in its faithfulness, its presence still availed behind the dense smoke as in every day before. Only the immediate experience changed perspective. Reality remained the same. The sun was there as always. Warmth and light, though obstruction prevailed. Haze crowded realities of the morning.

In that morning those many sunrises ago, surrounded by curtains of obscurity, a thought struck,

"The sun, though not visible, was, as in sunrises before, ever present."

Yes, in the awful unpleasant surroundings, although veiled, the sun prevailed. The celestial friend provided companionship, comfort, and contingency; regardless of billowing clouds. Momentary perspective simply did not reflect the truth surrounding me. At that moment, reality seemingly hidden was present. The initial unpleasant experience shrouded perspective, but truth won out at that moment. This was only temporary. Throughout that unpleasant smoke-filled day, a faithful companion accompanied as in every day before. Regardless of the visible situations in front of me that South African morning long ago, the sun in fact did present itself. It failed not. Taking confidence while struggling to breathe fresh air, I traveled not alone. In the haze, the sun rising occurred. Another truth appeared:

*"No matter how dark and murky the surroundings,
one is never alone as one might feel."*

Another pondering began to take hold, "Life is often like this. Life's hazes shroud perspective. Many souls seemingly exist in murky uncertainties. Day after day they fail to realize realties accompanying life's struggles. Struggles often cloud the true picture. Blurred uncertainties drive us into existences, not meant to live. Faith fades. Entanglements clutter as unpleasant days gone by engrain themselves into the fabric of our thinking casting ominous shadows.

A beautiful sunrise morning is what we often envision and expect. To live uncluttered, simplistic, and fulfilling. However, life often exists not in the realities of a morning's sunrise. Life habitually transpires in the haziness of difficulties, disappointments, and weariness. In sun risings from the east visited upon all inhabitants of this world, existence sometimes chokes on impurities surrounding us.

Hopelessness, despair, fear, and loneliness visits all at some point during life's journey. Usually visitations are multiple experiences through life. These visitations are temporary. The sun always rises and sets even during the most obscure of times. Truth arose again that day:

"In navigating life's challenges, there is always a companion regardless of felt distance or obscurity."

Son Risings seeks to help you discover your most valuable asset; your soul. Souls choked by smoky, hazy murk's of life can't enjoy the sunrise. Son Risings encourage you to make time in busy lifestyles to watch, wait, and anticipate life's Son Risings. In your soul, priorities can be set right. Anxieties are put at bay. Worry diminishes. Tired weary souls take on new life.

Son Rising's purpose is discovery. Taking time and giving care to the only part of us that will last forever; our souls. For those searching for new, better, and brighter risings, it is my hope this book offers encouragement. Souls viewing only fragments of sorrowful memories obstruct God's gift of life. Son Risings looks forward in hope and purpose. Most of all, Son Risings reminds that one is never as alone as one feels.

For those grappling to find satisfying risings of fulfillment, Son Risings is a humble attempt to rediscover your soul. As the Son rises in our souls, so may you experience purpose in life, regardless of smoky hazy obstructions surrounding you this day.

Ponderings

1. Where do your soul experiences occur?

2. Where's your special place to contemplate, consider, and take a soul's breath?

3. When do you take time for the real you?

4. What hazes cover your horizons of life?

5. How do you find the real you?

-3-
Meet the Real You
You are Your Soul

"The soul which has a body does not make two persons, but one human being."
Augustine – Johannis evangelium tractatus 19.15

Troubled Soul

In 1963, sitting with my mother in front of the TV, our family watched the procession of assassinated President JFK's lifeless body in horse drawn caisson. As a six-year-old, the entire event produced fear and anxiety. Wrestling with mortality sought parental assurances of safety and perpetuity. As six-year-old, I posed a pondering question, "Dad, who do, ah, how do I know, uh, that the devil won't get me when I die?" Dad's response, "I think you'll be ok, Buddy. Don't worry about it." Even at such a young age, my soul sought to discover both its terrestrial and celestial existence and continuity.

Catholic Soul

Raised in a Catholic background, there was much to value in my Catholic upbringing. The majestic presence of a cathedral, faithfulness of the Liturgy, respect for authority, and for me, the specialness of the Midnight Christmas Eve Mass brought a special sense of closeness to God. During my parochial schooling days of catechisms, First

Communion, and Confirmation, one heard much about the soul. Soul is heavily ingrained in the Church's liturgy and theology. Connecting my soul's existence with daily living proved opaque at best. For the Catholic part, I was baptized into the Church as an infant, supposedly, securing my soul. "Holy Baptism is the basis of the whole Christian life, the gateway to life in the Spirit."[2] Beyond that, my soul never surfaced in any personal practical considerations. It was secure in the Church, and cared for in Confession, Community, and the Eucharist. What more was needed? Practical soul consideration in the church existed seemingly only in soteriology, or the salvation experience. In the Catholic faith, Catholicism taught me that my soul was immortal, created by God.[3] In the "Church" my soul was secure forever.

Lost Soul

Then there was my good friend Lenny. After a lengthy discussion in 8th grade Study Hall, Lenny shared gently, "Don, your soul is lost." It was news to me. If it was lost, where did it go? Was it wandering around somewhere away from me? Did Lenny's words mean that somehow, life existed in some zombie existence until the soul was found? And, how could one recover their lost soul? Such terminology and descriptions confused and troubled my soul more than anything heard before. Lenny pressed, "Jesus will save your soul, if you put your faith in him." Asking more questions than Lenny was able to answer, I pressed, "So, my soul is not lost? It's just needs saving? Right?" The conversation continued for another hour into the lunch room. Lenny began to echo with the same pitch and tenor my of mother's response to regular onslaughts of questions, "Bud, I DON'T KNOW."

Those words that day, puzzled and concerned me beyond that Study Hall. Yes, I believed I possessed a soul, but I wasn't sure what "soul" meant. I concluded, "Well, maybe my soul is lost? Where is it, and how do I find it?" The whole thing kept a fifteen-year-old up many of nights contemplating possibilities. Thinking about a lost soul didn't make sense. One's soul either existed or it didn't. A soul was either here or not. How could it be lost?

Saved Soul

Visiting Lenny's Baptist Church, my soul confronted an eternal darkness outside of God without Christ. "Saved" became part of a new vocabulary. Saved marked the moment and point in time one decided to "Accept Christ." This secured one's soul for eternity in heaven. "Accepting Jesus, putting one's faith in Christ, asking Jesus into your heart, or just plain believing in Christ," marked new beginnings.

This is the point and moment when one was born again in Christ. Traditional churches refer to this as "decisional theology." Since it draws so many away from the "Church" towards Evangelicalism, decisional theology, a point in time where one "accepts Christ," is highly disfavored. Whatever called, that day way back in January of 1973 began a new direction in life supposedly pointing me towards Christ. Much of this new life was often directed towards church activities.

From my perspective in both movements, Catholic and Evangelicalism, the "soul" is rarely discussed beyond the salvation moment as each church defines it. Salvation guarantees a soul for eternity. How does that impact an individual now? American Christianity compartmentalizes the soul as part of the salvation to be experienced later in the heavenly realms. As one young man pressed me during counseling, "Yah, ok, I got that but what about my soul right now? I'm not over there yet, I am trying to get by right here. What about right now?"

Saved Lost Soul

Looking back, I often pondered, "Was that decision to get saved those many years ago a soul-connection with God, or an emotional people-connection?" After my soul got saved, training concerning the soul centered upon the "tripartite" nature of a person. Don't you just love heady theological words? "Tripartite" – so personal and up-close.

This is a very popular traditional teaching of the Church. "Man" possesses a body, spirit, and soul. This is what many theologians call the "trichotomy of man." After securing one's soul through baptism (Catholic) or decisional (Evangelical), most practical teaching, from my perspective, centered mostly upon one's body and spirit; the here now. Most soul-teaching seems concentrated on the celestial; or heaven. Very little focuses on terrestrial; right now. How do we deal with our souls today? Here and now?

Spirit-Care. Teaching on one's spirit accounted for individuality and personality. Here, according to teaching, a person's spirit is the sphere of God-consciousness.[4] Spirit is part of the nature of a person, the nature of man. The spirit of a person, was far more than just the air one

20

breathed.[5] A person's "spirit" is credited with emotional function. Whether a joyful spirit, sinful spirit, angry spirit, contented spirit, or whatever, somewhere in those descriptions my soul got lost; again.

Body-Care. Messages and teaching on how one should think, feel, act, react, reach out, repent, and forgive were the closest soul-care ever occurred. Occasionally a sermon on "Taking Care of Your Temple-Body" presented itself. After doing some rather loose math, I've figured I've been in over 1200 churches, listened to nearly 3,000 sermons, and preached a few thousand messages myself. The most isolated necessity left out of teaching was concerning the real you – your soul.

Maybe this is in part because western Christianity compartmentalizes the body, spirit, and soul to such an extent it fails to see practical daily soul-connectivity. Emphasis in both culture and church centers upon a temporary aging body inching towards cessation of breath. Soul teaching is directed solely towards a celestial, heavenly bound arrival. Rarely, is the terrestrial turbulent soul perspective – here and now much contemplated. In the business of church life many saved souls get lost.

Lost Saved Soul

An old Baptist Swedish Missionary in South Africa shared his predicament over a cup of Wimpy's[6] Coffee. He lamented his condition. Haggard and gaunt in his elderly years he whimpered, "It's as if I wasted my entire life. I've worked endlessly, but this is all I have to show for it? My soul is finished!" "Finished" is a common expression used in South African English expressing, "At one's complete end." Idolizing him at that time, I posed a pensive question, "What was it you were trying to accomplish?" His list included many wonderful admirable ambitions and accomplishments. What his answer did not include was any mention a soul-perspective. The soul-condition of this gracious honored old missionary slumped into a weakly discouraged confused existence. He gained much in ministry, much among his peers, much in his denomination, and much in accomplishments. Yet, none of that satisfied. While doing all the churchy stuff, the crescendo of his final words impacted deeply, "I came here to save souls, but I think I've lost mine."

His words were a strangely eerie repeat of John Wesley's, the Founder of Methodism, in the 18th century, "I went to America, to convert the Indians; but oh! who shall convert me? Who, what is He that will deliver me from this evil heart of mischief? I have a fair summer religion."[7] John Wesley, leader of the Great Awakening, seemingly soul-struggled too.

Hindu Souls

During many years in South Africa, I was privileged to know many devoted Hindus. I greatly admired their devotion and dedication. The Rama family befriended us after meeting Riga Rama during a Rotary International event. Sharing their Diwali Festival with us many times proved enjoyable. The Riga family explained that in Diwali, many lights are lit through the home and community. This signifies, as they explained to me, "inner light – the soul – triumph over darkness." Every member around their family table discussed at length the value of their soul that evening. The term "soul" came up quite often in discussions of daily life too. Believing in reincarnation, my Hindu friends believed one's body

22

discarded repeatedly as the soul put on a new body. In this, daily practical consideration of their soul was of high importance. They spoke of their soul often in daily reality.

Hindu's on a practical level appeared to talk more about the soul than any Christians I knew. Christians daily considerations of the soul seemed lost somewhere between church dogma and functionality.

Muslim Souls

Also, in Ladysmith, South Africa was a large South African Muslim population. During British expansionism into South Africa under the reign of Queen Victoria, many Indian servants provided services to the British soldiers in the field. Many Indians stayed in South Africa after the Boer War 1899 – 1902. Ladysmith became a center of Indian Hindus and Muslims alike. Mosques, temples, and churches peacefully coexist in Ladysmith even to this day.

Muslim business people in Ladysmith often shared their faith. One Muslim business man gifted me with a gold leaf Koran. During Ramadan, they often fasted. When asked as to the rationale for their fasting, a Muslim friend said, "Fasting is one of our pillars of faith. It's good for me to move my concentration away from my body and towards my soul during this time."

Zulu Souls

Serving as a missionary for twenty-two years among wonderful Zulu people in South Africa, Zulus often talked about their souls in daily realities. At the time, this was new to me. Zulu people didn't compartmentalize their soul into only a futuristic destiny. For many

Africans, soul is now. Soul is one's essence. Soul is the real you. Feelings came from a speaking soul. One Zulu teenager shared in a poem, "Umphefumulo wami kuwo yimi." **My soul is me.**

Zulu people use "soul" to describe a gamut of human experience. Soul talks of plight, disappointment, and suffering. Soul also speaks of love, joy, and exuberance. "Once an old man, telling of his suffering under the brutal Apartheid Government moaned, "Umphefumulo wethu wafa." **Our souls are dying.** The same Zulu man smiled peering deep into my eyes uttered, "Yet, this struggle also causes our souls to hope. Hope is life."

Once walking into the One-Hundred Bed Ward 1 in the Ladysmith Provincial Hospital, I approached the bedside of Mr. Bengu. The stench of gangrene permeated the air. My many trips to this African ward prepared me for the tragically common site of diseased ridden moaning people. In that ward, on that day, wreaking with the smell of gangrene, lay Mr. Bengu wreathing in pain, suffering double amputation of both his legs.

Mr. Bengu long struggled with diabetes. With limited ability and money, he grappled, as so many diabetics in Africa do, to obtain proper medications to control his affliction. It wasn't that Mr. Bengu didn't take his diabetes seriously. He just did not possess the means to combat the disease effectively. In his Zulu language, he moaned, *"My body is finished, but my soul still lives."* At age fifty-four, shortly after his amputation, Mr. Bengu died. As I conducted his funeral, his words repeated themselves, **"My soul lives."**

Those years among the Zulu people in South Africa witnessed too much pain and death; especially among children. Of the dozens and dozens of child funerals conducted, "soul" was the word of choice most often employed by grieving Zulu mothers. A precious Zulu mother fell on the casket of her only child crying, "Umphefumulo wami odabukile kabi!" *My soul is in great sorrow*. The song book of the Old Testament sings a familiar song, *"How long must I struggle with anguish in my soul, with sorrow in my heart every day?"* (Psalm 13:2)

Consoling another young tearful Zulu mother by the bedside of her young dying child she exclaimed, "Umphefumulo wami othembekile." *My soul is hopeful.* Confident souls too appeared at the most tragic and difficult of times among those wonderful African people. Their soul-resiliency amazed me.

American Souls

In America, Christian or not, often the meter of soul-health is directly measured to one's station of life. A soul does well if the body is healthy. "Your health is everything," the saying goes. If relationships satisfy, the soul is well. A big house – strong soul. Nice SUV – good soul. Biggest highest resolution screen TV – bright soul. Asking the health of a person's soul produces a confused answer, "I guess my soul is doing ok I mean, well, I'm doing ok. Yes, so I'm ok, my soul's ok. Ok?" American Consumerism seemingly offers a false barometer of soul-health. The more one possesses, the better the soul. Right?

Soul-health is also measured by one's perception of success. Yet, in one's success, soul consciousness evaporates in a haze of busy lives.

"Soul" becomes then a topic rarely discussed. It's reserved for philosophical or religious consideration only. Many hold an "I don't know" posture of their soul-consideration.

Then there is a growing number of Nihilists[8] who deny the soul's existence entirely. "Soul" is a word almost completely absent in daily American thought and conversation whether on secular, church, or philosophical levels.

Job's Soul

There's a guy in the Old Testament who lived about 6,000 years ago who suffered immense tragic losses. He has a lot to say about the soul. As Job examines the condition of his soul, he describes his plight. It is just one example of soul-condition in the Bible. Job's life didn't meet his expectations. Suffering a barrage of loses, he described his soul's existence as "bitter." Job mentions his extreme hardships and losses, *"And now my soul is poured out within me; Days of affliction have seized me."* (Job 30:16 NASB)

The phrase "bitter soul" resonated repeatedly as Lon spoke that Christmas Eve night. "Bitter-soul," it described much. People use many words to describe their dispositions. "I'm this or that," they say. But, perhaps, unknowingly they describe more than just how they feel. Maybe, they unknowingly speak to their soul's condition. Maybe, just maybe, what people are really saying is, "My soul is so very . . . this or that."

Where's the Soul?

A popular Wendy's commercial aired in the 70's. Two elderly women lifting the top bun off a hamburger at a competitor's restaurant looking at a postage stamp size burger demanded, "Where's the beef?" It's the sort of image popping into mind. Where's the soul? Where exactly is it? And, why don't we talk about it much if it's so important? Just where is the soul today in our teachings? Is it even important?

Great similarity here exists between Catholics, Traditionalists, and Evangelicals regarding the soul. Whether in baptism or decisional faith, the soul is rarely discussed outside of its origin and celestial destiny. The terrestrial journey, the here and now, rarely finds discussion and care. Enjoying many friends from Traditional to Baptist to Charismatic churches, soul conversation is not discussed outside an eternal-after-this life perspective. The soul is compartmentalized into two existences; before and after, lost or saved, before Christ or after Christ, with a soul or no soul.

Speaking with Lon that Christmas Eve, thoughts shot through my mind, "What's the condition of your soul right now?" Stressing only an eternal immortal view of Lon's soul ignored the immediate sitting before me. Lon's weakly soul cried out. Funny thing is, many of my friends over the years belonging to other faiths talked about their soul much more often than Christians. Almost daily. Yet, here sat Lon and myself in a Mega Church embarking on the conversation of his soul-care for the first time.

Ponderings

1. Which soul experience best describes you?

2. Describe your own self-care.

3. If someone asked you to describe your soul, what would you say?

4. How do you care for your soul?

5. Where's your soul? Right now?

-4-
Who Are You Really?
The Search for the Real You

"Never tell a child 'you have a soul.'
Teach him, you are a soul; you have a body."
George Macdonald, Annals of a Quiet Neighborhood

"It is hard to contend against one's heart's desire;
for whatever it wishes to have it buys at the cost of soul." [9]
Heraclitus

"And what do you benefit if you gain the whole world but lose your
own soul? Is anything worth more than your soul?"
Jesus

Jesus taught one's soul the most valuable part of a person. After our conversation, I pondered, "Just what's going on in Lon's soul?" The phrase "Soul-Care" entered my mind frequently. Remember thinking, "Lon how do you care for your soul? How much time do you give towards the real you compared to worrying, fretting, and whimpering about life's current road?" Finally, I asked, "Lon, what's going on in your soul here?" The question left him dumbfounded. No criticism or judgment. I've been there so many times myself.

Lon's description of his soul's condition echoed repeatedly. His soul survived in an uncared-for state. Choked by disappointment, worry, and station of life, his soul's condition affected and reflected every part of his being. The words of Jesus repeated themselves in my mind during our conversation, "What does any of this matter, Lon, if you lose your own soul?"

Democritus, the ancient Greek philosopher, is considered by many the "Father of Modern Science." His formulation of the Atomic Theory[10] stands out as one of his most astute and greater accomplishments. Concerning the soul, he wrote, *"Happiness resides not in possessions, and not in gold, happiness dwells in the soul."* The ancients recognized the importance of a healthy soul.

Soul Nephesh

The Bible is not completely concise about the nature of our soul.[11] There are three words in Jewish Hebrew thought used for "soul." The English word "soul" in the Old Testament section of the Bible is most often translated from the Hebrew word "nephesh."[12] In Jewish thought, nephesh is that aspect of the soul residing in the body.[13] English translations use different words in the Old Testament for "soul." Creature, being, living, person, thing, life, or animal are used depending on the context of the passage.

It is here some deny the immortality of a human soul. They cite bible verses equating animals and people on a level playing field regarding one's nephesh. Others argue that the soul is more of a mind-body connection.[14] "Most people don't agree on exactly what the "soul" is in English. Nonetheless, most people do agree on certain aspects: the soul is intangible, for example, and there's something mystical or unworldly about it."[15]

"Nephesh" occurs 754 times in the Old Testament[16] and literally means "living thing." The first four times "nephesh" is used in the Bible it refers to animals, indicating "breath of life." The word is first used in respect to humans Genesis 2:7, *"Then the LORD God formed the man from the dust of the ground. He breathed the breath of life into the man's nostrils, and the man became a living person."* Adam is literally a living "nephesh" or "soul." Some argue that Adam's nephesh points to a living mind and body. However, often when referring to people in the Bible "soul" often indicates the deepest, most intimate immortal part of a person.

In the New Testament, the word most often translated "soul" comes from the Greek word, "psyche." These two words, one Greek, one Hebrew, are most often translated "soul." They indicate the deepest most intimate core of a person. My spirit projects me. My soul is me. I am my soul.

Soul Care vs. Soul Talk

The purpose of Son Risings is not to engage in theological debate of the dichotomy or trichotomy view of body, soul, and spirit. Suffice it to say, the soul is the deepest immortal part of a person. While we are currently embodied in a temporary body, our souls are immortal. A renewed embodiment of the soul will occur again. (1 Corinthians 15:40) In this vein, consideration is given for the care the of the only immortal part of us that lives forever; our souls.

32

Self-Care vs. Soul-Care

Self-care is much bandied about these days. Taking care of the physical self finds multitudes of coaches, councilors, and trainers. Rightly so. We are embodied souls. Our bodies are not unimportant. Looking badly and feeling badly makes life laboriously unfulfilling. Much of self-care today focuses on seventy or eighty years one hopes to live in happiness, health, and peace. Good for them. Good for you. Take care of yourself. When you take good care of yourself, you take better care of all those connected to you in your relationships. Entrusted with a body, we are stewards of this housing during our brief vaporous existence on this earth.

Don't stop there. What about your immortal part? That part of you that will continue to exist long after your body transpires. The real you. What about your soul? How much care does the part of you that lasts far beyond your body's demise receive? Right now, this very moment, ask yourself, "How much time did I give my soul today?"

Son Risings, looks at the same seventy or eighty years. It goes further, beyond our temporary embodiment. There is the soul; you. The core. Your person more than just your mind and body's projection. Your soul; emotion, being, appetites, desires, and passions. Soul is the total you, the deep you, the immortal you. It's who you are. It's who you will always be; forever.

One's nephesh or psyche is far more valuable than just the body. Our bodies perhaps, enjoy one-hundred years of troubled life. Wellness emphasized in our culture focuses mostly on this decaying dying body. I know that sounds bleak. But, no one ever reversed the aging process through good self-care. At best, we just look and feel better until the end. Upon one's last breath, as our bodies finish, our beautiful God-created nephesh will live on. Doesn't wellness then demand focus upon nephesh?

Yes, Don, lose weight, exercise, get a yearly physical, and eat right. See a counselor if you need. Good things. But, what about the total you, Don? What about your soul? Right now, today, what are you doing to cultivate the total you? That troubled traumatized part of you? What are you doing to help that deepest part of your being? The forever part of your person? The special part of you? How much thought, time, and care does that get? How's your nephesh these days?

Until only a few years ago, outside of my spiritual disciplines of prayer and Bible reading, no time was given towards my soul. I was saved. I was serving. I was praying. I was reading the Bible. What more did it need? Perhaps there is just too much "I" in those few sentences. Maybe that was part of my struggle.

But, then the bottom dropped out. Years of witnessing some traumatic stuff in South Africa, horrible killings, and seeing dying, abused orphan children sent my mind and nephesh crashing. Diagnosed with Post Traumatic Stress Syndrome several years ago upon my return to the United States, marked my nephesh's awakening. An awakening that proved both good and bad. From the constant overload of traumatic suffering and death, my Christian Therapist, helped me put my emotional-rational world back in order. The reboot took over two years, and continues today.

Looking back not only at Africa, but to a six-year-old little boy hiding behind a curtain, nephesh suffered deep traumas. As his younger brother was beaten beyond an older six-year-old brother's ability to intervene, my nephesh was pushed to a breaking point. Can one's soul be broken? I think so. Mine was.

My neglected soul languished for years. Oh, my nephesh experienced God in Catholic Theology and Evangelical Born Againism. For this I am truly thankful. I value my experiences in both churches. Yet, nephesh failed to experience what Jesus promised, "Rivers of living water . . ." (John 7:38) As my Christian therapist led me to discovery and management of my PTSD, I too began to discover afresh my nephesh. In this epiphany, realization of the many contaminants I allowed entrance into my nephesh over the years began to emerge.

Soul Clutter

Once a Zulu man, living in abject poverty, asked me this question. "Are America souls pleasured?" Strange sounding question, but in his Zulu language it flowed nicely. He reasoned, since Americans possessed so much, their souls reflected the same fullness as their possessions. He reasoned, "The peoples of America 'obtain' so much, their souls must be very full." "Full" – an interesting word to describe a soul. My reply surprised the old Zulu man. "Yes, people in America possess much. Their souls are very full, but their souls also seem empty, unhappy, and discontent." His reply sobered the conversation, "Well, then perhaps their souls are filled with "mafuhlufuhlu?" The word he used in his Zulu language translates "rubbish" or "clutter." He continued, "If their souls are unhappy when they possess so much, what they possess is only clutter and not good for their souls." Quite a perspective from a poor African man struggling daily to survive. The old Zulu man seemed wealthier than richest people I know. And, I know a few.

Soul Neglect

Possession-laden people in First Worlds tend not to be the happiest people. This is particularly true for Americans.[17] Some studies indicate only one out of three Americans consider themselves happy.[18] How can people living in the wealthiest country of all human history struggle to find happiness? Is it perhaps, that while attending to the other things in life they miss the greater; their souls?

Over the course of almost forty years of pastoring and ministry, American Christians don't appear much happier than those outside the church. In fact, many of them, from my observations, are grumpy, complaining, faultfinding, self-righteous, and unpleasant beings. As they struggle with the same issues as their secular counterparts, they appear no better, and often worse. Many sessions with sincere Christian people over the years indicated empty, unhappy, discontent, wandering souls. Souls hearing a thousand Bible sermons didn't appear to experience the "rivers of living water" promised by the Soul-Shephard; Jesus. Spiritual maladies gave evidence to neglected souls.

Not only is there evidence of much personal neglect of the soul, but it is rare to hear many, if any, messages or conversations on soul care in the church as well. Perhaps, this accounts in part for the sea of unhappy discontent warring factions sitting in the pews of so many struggling small to medium size churches. Personal experience and countless conversations with discouraged pastors attest to the Pew-Wars in our churches. Members combating members. Perhaps these Pew-Wars are really soul-wars waged among congregants against themselves.

Soul Warfare

Peter, warned, *"Dear friends, I warn you as "temporary residents and foreigners" to keep away from worldly desires that **wage war** against **your very souls**."* (1 Peter 2:11) This Scripture is almost always applied to vices, wickedness, and bad behavior. Yet, doesn't trauma, injustice, worry, discontent, anger, and other spiritual disorders so common among Christians today wage war against the nephesh too?

There is a war out there. This war seeks to inflict permanent damage. This war is rarely discussed in our churches, small groups, and recovery groups. No criticism here. Sure, we talk about sin, habits, pornography, unforgiveness, relationships, vice, addictions, and more. Often, our approach to dealing with such challenges centers around presenting a spiritual, therapeutic deliverance from the immediacy of effects. As marriages and relationships continue to struggle, could it be that the solution lay deeper than just cognitive function? Could it be that answers lie deep within the inner tapestry of the soul?

In my American pastorates, constantly cranky, aggressive, caustic, hurtful, injurious, - enough adjectives? – assaulted my nephesh. I guess, because I carried the title "SENIOR PASTOR" small groups of ecclesiastical terrorists felt my nephesh a good place to run their lives aground into my very being. The debilitating experience, added to my diagnosed battle with PTSD produced the perfect storm. At times, I doubted my nephesh even real, loved, or cared for by God. In my head, theology assured that God cared. In my heart, I thought, "Really?"

I reassured myself continually. God's Word, the Bible, sprang to life. Yet, my soul struggled to see God's caring presence in the traumatic PTSD eruptions of my mind and soul. Then while journaling a personal realization occurred, "God saves my soul. It's my task, in part, to care for my soul."

I began looking closely at the character of my soul. Soul construction became the priority as I reordered my life. What might cure a heavily, troubled, PTSD traumatized angry soul? Are there soul-cures? What might soul-care look like? Does soul-comfort exist, and can it be obtained? If so, how? What are the soul-catalysts for a better healthier soul? This marked redirection in my journey.

Perhaps, there is help and encouragement here for you too. Maybe, not. For deeply probing theological minds, you will most likely find this work incomplete and lacking. Theological minds often can't help finding fault and criticism in myriads of theological positions out there today. My purpose is not to debate the theological nature of the soul. That has been done ad nauseam. In that world, there is debate, disagreement, and argument. As debates by theological focused clergy continue, multitudes of nephesh languish and perish. People in the pews care little for such things. Their cares center pragmatically on making life work. How then can life work if centered upon a weak misdirected sickly soul?

Much of ministry these days seems more about managing people than soul-care. My journey takes me often to pastors and missionaries whose souls crash upon the rocks of "ministry." It also converses with the many "injured" members of those ministries. Their tribe is numerous and growing every day. As members of the Church, they choose to leave the church to join another tribe. Their stories are often heart wrenching experiences of serving till running dry. Working in the church while running on empty, or suffering under a celebrity driven personality.

A gifted young pastor, part of a mega-church, expressed, "If this is the church you can have it. My soul wants to be part of **the Church; not that church**." One of the most gifted young speakers I've ever heard, left the staff of that church rarely to return to a local congregation. Speaking with me many times about his journey, he shared of an ever-growing assembly of wounded Christians who love **"The Church but not that church."** They make up the "Universal Church of Jesus Christ" meeting in small groups, in digital settings, and in homes. They believe the organized over programed performing church is out of touch with nephesh. Is it possible in all of this we are out of touch with ourselves too?

Focusing upon the immortal part of you; your soul is the true journey. For me, it's deeply personal taken from the many pages of my journal during the turbulent three years of my diagnoses of Noncombative Cumulative PTSD induced by witnessing a hundred bloody deaths in the killing fields of Natal South Africa. In learning to manage my PTSD, my soul began to heal. The journey taught me to look afresh at my nephesh. In thanking God for my rugged journey every day, I began to see the Son Rising again.

It brings me to a place in which I can openly share. My Son Risings offers hope to weary, tired, bitter, anguished, heavy, and wounded nephesh. Come along. Let me share with you my discoveries. While perhaps not new discoveries, they are in fact new to me. And, perhaps, maybe, in the pages ahead lay a few discoveries for you too.

-5-

Soul-Checkup
How's Your Soul Doing?

"I will search my soul and ponder the difference now."
Asaph, Psalm 77:7

"But souls can't be sold. They can only be lost and never found again."
Ray Bradbury, Long After Midnight

Once a long-standing church member stormed into the office twenty minutes before Sunday morning service. Always trying to hide from the discontent, angry, or complaining on Sunday mornings, he prevailed that day. Nothing deflates a heart ready to share a message of encouragement with 500 people more than an assault of critical verbiage 10 minutes before church. There stood the man in his normal critical agitated state. It was not our first encounter. He blurted out, "CAN I TALK WITH YOU FOR A MINUTE?" Anticipating his regular homily of complaints, I approached the most difficult man from a soul perspective. Looking up from my desk, I asked, "What is ill with your soul?" Caught off guard, he began to mumble. Here, this previous elder, Bible teacher, and leader drooled, "Well, good, I guess. I accepted Jesus in my heart many years ago. So, yah, you betcha, I'm good." Passing by him through the open door of my office, I replied, "Good for you!" Stunned, he stood emotionless as I proceed to the Second Service already well underway.

Throughout the Old and New Testament, the condition of individual's nephesh is described in remarkable contrasts. Both dashed and joyful nephesh transparently present themselves in the lives of the people in the Bible. From these Scriptures are recorded a variety of soul-afflictions and adulations that remarkably identify with us thousands of years later. It's what makes the Bible such a remarkably contemporary book.

Soul-care requires one take a long diagnostic look at one's own nephesh. It begs the question, "What is the condition of my soul?" Before a doctor treats a sickly person, that physician must ascertain what afflicts an individual. A good report indicates one carries on in their current practices. A negative report demands course correction. Accurate prognosis requires an understanding of condition, cause, and cure. Many individuals visited in the pages of the Bible reveal much about their soul's conditions.

Soul-Emptiness

Hannah, a mother approaching the end of child bearing age goes to the Temple. She despaired her childless state. Her nephesh missed something; children. She cried out! "She poured out her soul (nephesh) before the LORD." (1 Samuel 1:15) The Hebrew word translated "pour" is also translated in the Old Testament as "dump" or "gush." Hannah dumped her heart out before God. Her painful soul gushed out. She opened the flood gates of her troubled soul. Hannah's soul seemed exiled from God due to her childless state.

Her state left more than just yearning for offspring. In the Ancient world, barren women marked many perceived ills. "Barrenness" pointed towards some personal deficiency. Infertile women experienced social sigma and isolation. Infertility indicated spiritual deficits or punishment for sin. During my many years among the Zulu people, infertility often marked a belief that one displeasured one's deceased family members referred to as ancestors. During my years of pastoring in the United States, couples often asked, "Why doesn't God give us children? Why doesn't God answer our prayers. What have we done wrong? What are we doing wrong?" Two completely different cultures believed infertility to some degree marked a deficiency on their part.

Beyond the social stigma, barrenness in the ancient world also threatened a women's financial security. Children, especially males, assured an old woman's survival. There were little provisions made for the elderly outside the establishment of family. Hannah looked at her older years advancing with great uncertainty, fear, and dishonor.

She cried pouring out her soul during public worship in the women's quarter of the Temple. Her pouring out drew the attention of the highest religious person of Israel's day; the High Priest. Hannah's soul-gushing resembled the utterances and behaviors of an intoxicated individual. Eli, the High Priest, accused her of coming to worship staggering drunk! How often do we fail recognize the gushing of an individual's soul as a cry for help? In our busy churches, soul-empty people attend worship services only to leave as empty as they entered.

Do, we the church, fail to read accurately the gushing dumping of empty souls entering the church looking for God? Hannah's incoherent emptying of her soul cried out for help in the very place help supposedly existed.

The great part about this story, is that God responded. Hannah's prayer is answered when Samuel is born. Samuel became one of the most positive influences among his people. Hannah's soul brimmed with confidence and fulfillment! Through a long and painful journey, God rescues her soul.

Soul-Bitterness

Six thousand years ago, Job enjoyed the highest standing in his community. His large family, large ranch, large farm, many servants, and beautiful wife marked Job as a wealthy man. He was admired and respected. Job enjoyed a unique relationship and standing with God. He had it all. Everything! And, God liked him too on top of everything else. He lived the "perfect" life. Happy in the most idyllic sense. Sort of makes you sick doesn't it. The guy had everything. That was until that day.

Have you experience a "that day?" A phone call that changes your life. "Is this Mr. _____? I'm sorry to tell you that your _____ was _____." Or, the "that day" when the doctor's report came back announcing the horrible "C" – cancer. That day when your company sells, and the merger means downsizing. To no fault of your own, you lose your job. Or, the Housing Market crash of 2008 happens. You lose your house. Or, on your death bed, one of your adult children refuses to talk with you. A car accident. A sickness. Loss of social standing. The doctor informs you that your carrying an STD given to you by your spouse. Betrayal. A phone call from your oldest son, "Dad, I woke up and went into the baby's room." Another loss. Another lie. Another disappointment. Too much criticism. A midlife shift to the bad. A team that showed so much promise just to disintegrate before your very eyes for no quantifiable explanation. You know, the "that day" which changes your life forever.

Job experienced one of those days to the extreme, almost six thousand years ago. In one day, four different messengers delivered devastating horrific news. The first messenger arrived at Job's home one afternoon announcing, *"Your oxen were plowing, with the donkeys feeding beside the oxen, when the Sabeans raided us. They stole all the animals and killed all the farm hands. I am the only one who escaped to tell you."* (Job 1:14-15) Job, you've lost your job! You can't farm any longer and produce income. You can't feed your family any longer! Bad people took your farm from you. **People did this to you, Job!**

A second messenger arrived before the first messenger finished telling Job the horrible news. The newly arrived messenger announces, *"The fire of God has fallen from heaven and burned up your sheep and all the shepherds!"* (Job 1:16) **Job, God did this to you!** He took your ability to produce clothing and income for your family!

While the first and second messengers were still speaking, Job must of thought, "Oh great, here's a third messenger! Don't tell me! What else has happened now!" The third messenger informed Job of more devastating news, *"Three bands of Chaldean raiders have stolen your camels and killed your servants. I am the only one who escaped to*

45

tell you." (Job 1:17) Job is now bankrupt and penniless. **Job! Your enemies did this to you!**

During my ten wonderful years of serving as a Fire Chaplain with the Eagan Fire Department and Grand Rapids Fire Department, both in Minnesota, I comforted people who lost everything in fires. One man shared as I stood with him watching firefighters battle a fire gutting his home, "Well, the important thing is my family is safe. At least we got out." Job did not enjoy such comfort.

As the first three messengers described the respective catastrophes, a fourth messenger arrived. Fearing perhaps to tell his master the news the servant begins, *"Your sons and daughters were feasting in their oldest brother's home. Suddenly, a powerful wind swept in from the wilderness and hit the house on all sides. The house collapsed, and all your children are dead."* Job they're all gone. Every one of them. Not a single living offspring is left for you to love and carry on your name. There will be no grandchildren and joyful playing with them in your elder years. Job, who did this to you!? Why has this happened to you Job? What changed God towards you Job? There must be a reason. There must be an answer. The must be a shortcoming somewhere in all of this. No one, Job, has this bad of luck! **You did this to yourself, Job.**

Job's reactions reflected his uniquely close relationship with God. Devastated, *"Job stood up and tore his robe in grief. Then he shaved his head and fell to the ground to worship."* (Job 1:20) To worship? Are you kidding me? Yes, Job worships. In utter grief he cried out, *"Everything I had God gave me. I entered this world naked, and we all leave naked. God* chose to take it all away. I will praise the name of the LORD anyways!" (My paraphrase) Job responded well. Job said it right. Prayed it right. It couldn't get any worse? Right? Hang on.

Job's friends and the community initially rallied around him, but soon they began to ask, "Hum, I wonder why God is doing this to Job? There must be a reason. Who was at fault here? Their theology did not include a God of Fairness to allow such harsh circumstances to fall on a person if their life was in order. "Job," they asked, "Why is God punishing you? You must find your sin and confess it." Thanks Job's friends! You're such an incredible . . .

Friends did little to aid the grieving Job. As is often the case with many of God's people through the ages, they tried to lay blame for Job's personal losses. Something deep within us searches for the "Why" to every dilemma. A blame for bad fortune. Job's friends concluded that God orchestrated all Job's calamities' due to his spiritual deficiencies. "Job, somewhere you sinned, making God very angry with you. Think about it Job. Where did you sin?" As friends accused, Job's wife joined the fray. *"Are you still trying to maintain your integrity? Curse God and die."* (Job 2:9)

Years ago, our son Daniel once again found himself in an intensive care room struggling for life with a strange autoimmune system disease. As he battled for life, a well-meaning Christian friend probed, "Do you think God is maybe trying to tell you something here?" People say the stupidest things, don't they? Tired, wearied, and concerned for my ten-year-old son, I unkindly shot back, "Well, I tell you what, if He does tell me something, I'll let you know. How about that?"

This marked perhaps Job lowest point. Job cried out, *"I am disgusted with my life. Let me complain freely. My **bitter soul** must complain."* (Job 10:1) The word "bitter" here is also used in the Old Testament to describe food too bitter to eat. Job's staggering losses created bitter unpalatable bits and pieces of life. His bitterness tainted every other consideration of life. He complained. Not all complaining is negative. Here, God received Job's complaints because they expressed his harsh realities of life.

As a little kid, up in Minnesota, we used to pick apples from Mrs. Gunderson's trees next store. Impatient, we picked those apples while still green and immature. The sourness of those apples made them most unpalatable. We ate Mrs. Gunderson's apples with heavy doses of salt. Those sour, bitter apples upset our tummies. Nothing made those apples edible in their raw state.

Our years in South Africa introduced us to new and unusual foods. Some South Africans enjoy a beef spread paste called Brovil. This black beef paste or jam is incredibly bitter. Invited for a get together with some South Africa friends to welcome us to South Africa, we gathered at a friend's home. Laid out before us was a potluck of South African culinary specialties. A chocolate covered cake caught my eye. I took a small sample of every entrée as not to offend anyone. Arriving at that mouthwatering chocolate covered cake, a healthy piece found its way to my plate.

My brain processed to my taste buds the anticipated chocolate sensation. Working through the healthier choices first, finally with a hot cup of coffee, the moment of delightful encounter arrived. As I put the first morsel of chocolate covered savor in my mouth, oral confusion and disbelief confronted me. Trying not to show a disapproving face, my brain said, "What is this horrible black bitter taste? This is not sweet! This is not frosting! The is spoiled rotten something. What is it? It's so incredibly bitter! WHAT IS IT?" A newly acquainted South African friend sensed the dilemma. "Not chocolate icing is it Don?" as he bellowed. "Ah, well, no, not really," I replied. Politely I asked, "What is this on top?" Replying with a continued chuckle, "It's Brovil." As not to offend everyone, the next thirty minutes were spent choking down that concoction of bitter beef extract. Funny thing is, I got to where I enjoyed this black bitter paste on the proper foods in very small doses.

Job's life continued in the most bitter of unpleasant ways after suffering his devastating losses. A friend of mine shared her story on Facebook. It resembles Job. She shared,

> So many thoughts going through my head as I start this day. It is the 4th anniversary of our son's home-going to Jesus. The one thought that keeps coming to me is GOD'S LOVE for me! Travelling from Indiana to Wisconsin that day to be with our 4 grandchildren who were suddenly without parents (their mom was ill and unable to be with them), I found myself distraught and sobbing beside a sink in a tollway plaza restroom. Several women passed by me, oblivious to my emotional distress.

Another longtime friend has suffered immense loses. His eight-year-old son, grabbed his head crying in pain during recess at school thirty years ago. Within twenty-four hours he was dead from a brain aneurism. Some years later his oldest son developed cancer. For two decades, his son battles this disease. Upon the very week of his retirement, my friend's wife suffered a debilitating stroke. Since retirement, two grandchildren have died of cancer. If you are in this elite class of Loss-Sufferers, you perhaps understand bitterness of soul.

This "bitter" is used here by Job to describe worst-case outcomes of life. Bitter marks Job's life and his lowest of lows. Job's bitter soul brings him to a disgustingly self-loathing complaining existence. Can you blame him? Do you know any Job's? Perhaps, that complaining bitter, unhappy person you work with suffers from soul-bitterness due to staggering personal losses. Soul-bitterness casts ominous shadows on many aspects of life.

Soul-Wounding

Many carry wounded souls. Again, Job cried out, *"And the souls of the wounded cry out; . . ."* (Job 42:12 NASB). Some of the sweetest words in the Bible attests to healing of wounded souls. *"He heals the brokenhearted and binds up their wounds."* (Psalms 147:3 NASB) The word "brokenhearted" is from the Hebrew word "shabar." When used in the Hebrew Niphal stem it carries the idea to be broken, maimed, crippled, or wrecked.[19] The heavy emphasis here is upon "broken." It is alarmingly interesting that my journey these days meets with so many broken people wounded by events, circumstances, or some exchange of words or events with other Christians. Crushed and broken describes accurately these wounded souls.

Serving almost ten years on two fire departments in Minnesota both as a firefighter and chaplain, I attended several incidents where people suffered horrible crush wounds. Crushing of the body is one of the most horrible sights witnessed on emergency scenes. Crushing maims, disfigures, and brings harsh pain with difficult new realities to a person's life. Some crushed people encountered on those emergency scenes remind me of soul-crushed people hobbling through life.

During my second American pastorate, Dave who rarely attended church, showed a disdain for pastors. Dave didn't care, like, or trust most pastors. Upon learning from Dave's son, the betrayals and deception perpetrated upon his father by a pastor, a wounded soul emerged. Dave's disfigured soul simply didn't allow trust towards pastors. There was no room for consideration in Dave's life for another chance. There was never a chance at relationship with Dave. As Dave put it to this pastor one day, "That pastor crushed any possibility of trusting you pal!"

A woman in the same church shared another incredible story with a much better ending. With four children, her husband abandoned her up in Northern Minnesota many years ago. With no job skills or money, she was destitute. As she described it, "His abandoning us crushed me and my family deeply." The wounding of her soul deeply affected her for many years. Fortunately, with much prayer, trust in God, fortitude, and determination, she started a small store way up in Northern Minnesota. She named her new convenience store God's Country. Her small business supports her extended family. As she described her story, the words of David, the ancient king of Israel, came to mind. *"The LORD is near to the brokenhearted and saves those who are crushed in spirits."* (Psalms 34:18 NASB) She encourages many single moms in that Northern Minnesota area to not give up hope.

Soul-Despair

In the Old Testament, there is an ancient collection of songs. We refer to these songs as Psalms. There are one hundred and fifty in all. In the forty-second Psalm, the song writer sings, *"O my God, my soul is in despair within me."* (NASB) The individual who wrote this Psalm withdrew himself from people, community, and worship. In his Psalm, he asks a diagnostic question, *"Why are you in despair, Oh my soul?"*

Once, a woman in my congregation approached me after the Sunday morning message. The passage I taught was from the forty-second Psalm. The young slightly perplexed woman asked, "You mean people who lived way back then suffered from depression and despair too?" In the local dialect of Noorden Minnesootaha, I answered, "You Betcha!"

The Sons of Korah were leaders of song and worship in the Temple in Jerusalem under King David in the Old Testament. They led throngs of people in worship regularly. Many of the songs written in these Psalms perhaps emanated from observing the conditions of Hebrew people coming to the Temple for worship. A wide array of spiritual conditions and emotions apparently confronted these worship leaders. They write often to the human condition of the soul.

Imagine coming to the Temple suffering a great personal loss. A child has just died. Hail blighted a crop ready to harvest. Family finances wiped out completely. Sickness befalls your family. Depression lurks in the recesses of your person. As you approached the Temple in your grief-stricken condition you hear these Sons of Korah singing, *"Why, my soul, are you downcast? Why so disturbed in me? Put your hope in God, for I will yet praise him, my Savior and my God."* Psalms 42:5 (NIV)

The word translated "despair" or "disturbed" comes from the Hebrew word "shachach." It is translated in our English Bibles in a variety of ways. The King James Version uses the phrase "cast down." Why are you cast down my soul? "Shachach" literally refers to a bowing down or prostrating one's self in a crouching manner. In this sense, the word implies an experience of being brought into a low place or estate in life.

During many visits to Ventura, California, I couldn't help but notice all the homeless people in the area. More than once, approaching a homeless person, I asked, "What contributed to your current state in life?" One man standing in tattered clothing, unshaved, unbathed, and unkempt replied, "I used to have it all, but now I am brought to this low place because of my drinking." By "low place" he referred to the community living under the bridge off Victoria Avenue. The man clearly lived a crouching life filled with despair.

In both Psalms forty-two and forty-three, the same song writer cried of suffering from a downcast soul filled with despair. The Sons of Korah describe in detail. Here are their observations of crouching despaired filled souls.

Abandonment. In both Psalms, a question is repeated numerous times, *"Where is this God of yours?"* In despair, often one doubts God's goodness and provision. In a soul-despair stricken state, the song singer cries out, "Why have you forgotten me?" A feeling of abandonment worsens with the phrase, "Why have you tossed me aside?" (Psalms 43:2) Can you remember a time when you wondered, "God are you really there?"

Just last week, I conducted the funeral of a beautiful young woman who took her own life. Her distraught mother asked, "Where is God now?" No one could find reason or sense in this young thirty-year-old mother of two ending her life. What added to the search for reason where over 300 young adults who attended the funeral. She seemingly was surrounded by friends. Over hearing another conversation around the corner at the funeral home, abandonment expressed itself again, "You'd think God might have done something. She was so young and beautiful."

A few months ago, I enjoyed the pleasure of speaking at the Milwaukee Rescue Mission in Milwaukee, Wisconsin. My father served many downtrodden men there for many years when the old mission was on 3rd Street in downtown Milwaukee. During my short message, the emphasis was upon the goodness of God. Many men came afterwards for prayer. One very old man made his way towards me. With a hard-German accent looking straight into my eyes, he bellowed, "Look at me! Do you see any of God's goodness here?" Before uttering another word, he turned and shuffled away; abandonment.

Punishment. Once speaking with a missionary, he described his plight. Just about everything and anything that could go wrong in his ministry, did go wrong. Having suffered a disappointing refusal for Visa Renewal in the first country he served, he now stood with me looking at a mountain in another country. He thought about "packing it up again." Describing his many misfortunes, he sighed, "I just wonder what I've done wrong, and what God is doing to me here? Like God's punishing me for something."

It seems common to feel a sense of punishment or abandonment when one's soul languishes in despair. Speaking with a dejected pastor forced to resign his church as Senior Pastor, he sighed, "Seems like I've been tossed aside; again. And, where is God in all of this? I don't know. I just don't know." Perhaps this is the reason only one in ten pastors retire as a pastor.[20]

In encouraging many believers, a sort of Christian Agnosticism often emerges, "Yes, there is a God, but because of the circumstances of my life, if He is there, He can't really care much about me. That is if He's even out there at all." This thought and sentiment is alarmingly common among many tribes of people who used to attend church. They cry out like the Sons of Korah, *"Why have you forgotten me?"* (Psalm 42:9)

Grief. Soul-despair carries another dark mark; grief. This song writer cries out, "Why must I wander around in grief." (Psalms 42:9) The word "grief" comes from the Hebrew word "qadar"[21] and carries the idea of mourning. Literally the idea here is to be dark or black as in a storm approaching. In 1 Kings 18:45, the same word is used to describe a coming storm, *"And soon the sky was black with clouds."* Job used "qadar" when describing his life, *"I walk in gloom, without sunlight."* Do you know anyone like this? Like Winne the Pooh's Eeyore, whose dumpy gloomy, pessimistic words overshadowed every situation no matter how cheery, soul-grief people justifiably see a black cloud in every silver lining. To them, nothing is good, nothing brings hope, and all is without beauty.

Another word used in the Old Testament for grief is "tuwgah." When the English word "grief" is translated from "tuwgah" it often refers to an extreme heaviness of soul. The worship leader cries out, *"My soul weeps because of grief."* (Psalm 119:28 NASB) Grieving people suffering from immense losses experience a wearing down of their soul. A weeping disposition often marks them. I've learned to look deeper into these people's lives before writing them off as whiners or gloomy. Their stories tell of a journey of losses. Sometimes incredibly so.

Exploitation. I paid attention to a pair of aging sisters. Their demeanor identified with these words, *". . . And the souls of the wounded cry out."* (Job 24:12 NASB) The word for cry here is often translated "groan" in other Bible versions. Groaning aching souls is the picture that came to mind with these two sisters.

Close observation brought me to a possible reason for these two sisters' soul-maladies. Occasionally seeing their aging father, I'd shake his hand, inquiring to his health. During our usually short conversation, I'd also enquire, "How are your daughters doing?" Every time he turned pale, stuttered, and ended the conversation. The question saw him ending up in the ER at the local hospital immediately afterwards. Possibilities of some traumatic events showed themselves apparent.

Oppression. Soul-despaired people often suffer from oppression. During my years in South Africa, from 1986-2006, I witnessed vicious oppression during the Apartheid era. As an eye witness to some of the brutalities of the National Party upon the peoples of color in South Africa, oppression often led to much grief. The worship leader sings, *"Why must I wander around in grief, oppressed by my enemies?"* (Psalms 43:2)

Privileged to live near oppressed people in South Africa under the brutal fist of Apartheid, oppression occurred daily. The distresses and pressures put upon all people of color during this dark period of South African history produced heavy soul-laden people. As Simon Dube, an elderly Zulu man, often reminded me, "We blacks are suffering here in South Africa." And, suffer they did. Prayer meetings among the Zulu people those many years ago were prayers of petition before God for deliverance and hope during grievous suffering.

Oppression tragically finds root in many families here in the United States too. During my ten-year tenure pastoring in the United States, story after story of familial abuse opened another oppressive world. Some of the stories came from adult women well into midlife years. Their stories told of sexual exploitation experienced during adolescent and teenage years. I saw soul-similarities between these American women and the Zulu people in South Africa. Two completely different cultures, both living in soul-despair due in large part to oppression forced upon them. One woman shared, "The things that my father and his brothers did to me changed me. I know I am a dark, gloomy person, but that is the person I've always been since those things happened to me."

Doctor's Prescription

Most times when visiting my doctor for a checkup, he prescribes a course of action. Lose some weight, get your blood pressure under control, and reduce stress. Reducing my weight by forty pounds, did significantly lower my blood pressure. Pretty incredible, huh?

The Bible offers many prescriptions for aiding one's soul. When in despair, the soul speaks out. God speaks out too. In Psalm thirty-five, King David's back is against the wall. The pressures of leading a struggling nation surrounded by enemies seeking to destroy them cry out, *"Then my **soul will rejoice** in the LORD and delight in his salvation."* (Psalm 35:9 NIV). David speaks while in extreme anxiety and stress. In soul-despair, he looks forward to the LORD. LORD often pronounced as "Adonai" rather than by its literal name, signifies "master" or "owner." David sees God as the best remedy to his soul's dilemma. In fact, David views God as the only permanent cure.

Ponderings

1. How's your nephesh doing these days?

2. What soul-despair events are occurring in your life?

3. When, if ever, did you experience, soul-emptiness?

4. When has your soul experienced:

- Abandonment?

- Punishment?

- Exploitation?

- Oppression?

5. What's the best remedy for any of your soul's dilemma?

-6-
Soul-Loss
Missing the High Note

"Don't sell your soul to buy peanuts for the monkeys."
Dorothy Salisbury Davis

"And what do you benefit if you gain the whole world but lose your own soul?"
Jesus

A brief examination of Jesus famous words in Mark 8 and Matthew 16 warns of losing one's soul. Jesus words, ***"And what do you benefit if you gain the whole world but lose your own soul?"*** ranks as one of the top most important verses in the Bible. A read of the entire narrative gives a clearer picture:

Then Jesus began to tell them that the Son of Man must suffer many terrible things and be rejected by the elders, the leading priests, and the teachers of religious law. He would be killed, but three days later he would rise from the dead. As he talked about this openly with his disciples, Peter took him aside and began to reprimand him for saying such things. Jesus turned around and looked at his disciples, then reprimanded Peter. "Get away from me, Satan!" he said. "You are seeing things merely from a human point of view, not from God's." Then, calling the crowd to join his disciples, he said, "If any of you wants to be my follower, you must give up your own way, take up your cross, and follow me. If you try to hang on to your life, you will lose it. But if you give up your life for my sake and for the sake of the Good News, you will save it. And what do you benefit if you gain the whole world but lose your own soul? Is anything worth more than your soul? If anyone is ashamed of me and my message in these adulterous and sinful days, the Son of Man will be ashamed of that person when he returns in the glory of his Father with the holy angels." (Mark 8:31-38)

Christ spoke these words to both his disciples to a crowd nearby. The Twelve claimed to follow, know, and love him. No one was closer to Jesus than Peter, James, and John. During Christ's announcement of his death, Peter sort of flips out on Jesus. Peter, alarmed at Jesus expectation, "takes Jesus aside." Close study seems to indicate that Peter possibly physically accosted Jesus pulling him aside. Peter then lays into the Son of God on the feasibility of his plan. Try to picture the whole scene for a moment. Can you image grabbing your employer by force, pulling him or her to the side, and reprimanding the person in front of a large group? Jesus responds.

His soul-warnings were particularly directed towards Peter. Jesus severely rebuked Peter in the strongest of terms. Obliterating Peter Jesus slams back, "Yes, you were the only one to walk on water with me, your standing here like a big shot tearing into me, but hey Peter, my friend, Get THEE behind me Satan! Be careful of losing your soul in this whole thing. Your soul, Peter, is the highest consideration." And, "John, you are my favorite, but be careful. You to my friends, be careful. What does any of your god-pursuits matter if you lose your souls in pursuing it?" Imagine Peter's pain at Jesus' words towards him.

Closer study of the passage indicates that Peter revolted at the mention of Christ's death. A question presents itself, **"Is it possible for people deeply committed to God to lose their souls in church, leaving them dry, empty, and unfulfilled?"** Jesus' teaching to his disciples here seems to indicate that possibility. Churches today may in fact be filled with lost soul church members.

Jesus continues, **"If you try to hang on to your life, you will lose it."** (Mark 8:36a) Hanging on appeared as in our day today the trait of that day. Hanging on to my money. Hanging on to my position. Hanging on to my expectation. Hanging onto my structure. Hanging onto my desire. Hanging on to the way we always did church the last thirty years. Hanging on to whatever I decide to hang onto above other higher considerations seems the point here. I think most of us plague ourselves with hanging onto our desires to the detriment of our souls. Hanging onto our lives prevents us from taking up our crosses daily and following Christ. A recent experience may help us grab hold of this whole losing of one's soul.

Our Trumpet Dilemma

Currently, a pastor friend of mine shares his church's transition. Desperately needing to transition their Baby Boomer music in his church to a more connecting musical approach towards Millennials presented a daunting task. Their current music program is led by no less than One Director, fifty Boomers in the choir, ten more Boomer worship singers, a Boomer pianist, Boomer keyboards, a Boomer Country Western bass player, a Boomer guitar rocker, Boomer trumpets, trombones, clarinets, violins, and more. All this produces a noisy upbeat late eighties music style by people in their late sixties. This music style was enjoyed by Boomers twenty-five years ago, who overthrew their parents during the Church Music Uprisings. Now these Boomers resist any diversion from their musical tastes. They call it "Christian Music." That's how I developed my definition of Christian music. Christian music is, "Whatever I like best."

Play that Trumpet!

American Boomers don't seem to understand or care that they no longer make up the largest population group in America. Apart from any other consideration, that Boomer worship team held their ground, "We play our trumpets; period." As those brass instruments missed their notes repeatedly, every Sunday, the rather noisy confused jumbled assortment needed change; badly. Standing out in the dustup was a seventy-year-old trumpet player. Believing himself Doc Severisen on the Tonight Show with Johnny Carson in the 70's and 80's, this old church trumpeter attempted high note after high note in every worship set. Rarely did he hit those high notes. Like stepping on a cat's tail, the squeal was painful. Regardless, nothing abated his music prowess. It was painful. Reminded me of several root canals I've had done over the years. The music did anything but, prepare people for worship and the Sunday message. A compromise was offered.

In the first service at 9:00, things would continue as usual. Every Boomer that wanted could play in that service. Doc, play that trumpet! Gray hairs, sing with those Grand Canyon vibratos! Sing with your deep concentrative painful facial grimaces. Yep, that's what everyone wants to see on Sunday morning. And, what you we call this? All together now. WORSHIP! Enjoy. The grey hairs will rule the first service. Help yourself Boomers. It's your time. But, in the second service, things must change. There are other people in this church besides over 50's. The church needs to attract younger people into sharing, serving, and singing. And, besides, where will most you Boomers be in ten to fifteen years from now? To be brief about it, that all depends.

No Other Trumpets Allowed

A younger team, Millennials, will lead in worship second service. Need to bring some young adults into the church. Something for everyone. Yes, they're not as committed as Boomers. Those Millennials don't give money like we Boomers do. That's ok, because we can help them mature and grow. They will eventually get it. Ok? Great! Right? Everyone on board? Yes, no? What? "Ah, well, pastor wait a minute here. No, we Boomers are not on board. We don't like this!" A soul sickness prevailed over some in that "Worship Team." Members murmured in the dark church's corners, "If I can't play my trumpet in both services I'm leaving this church I've belonged to for the past thirty years." Doc is taking his trumpet elsewhere. We Boomers will lose our souls over this! Seeking to hang onto their trumpets, some lost their souls. Departing souls played their favorite trumpet tune, "I Asked Jesus in My Heart." Reassuring themselves of their Jesus Prayer years ago, their souls sang walking out the doors, "Since Jesus came into my heart, I'll play my trumpet anyway I want now."

Certainty, as a Boomer, my read of my generation is that we are the most privileged spoiled self-centered generation to ever walk the planet. Boomers hold most the wealth and power. That will change. It is changing. Many Boomers seek to save their lives, their ways, and wants above every other generation after them. This is particularly true in church. I'm going to play my trumpet no matter what!

Losing Your Trumpet in Church

But Doc, *"What do you benefit if you gain your trumpet, but lose your own soul? Is that trumpeting worth more than your soul?"* Doc, playing that trumpet in both services on Sunday, missing every high note you attempt, is it worth it? Really? REALLY?? How do you play for God with that kind of attitude?

It was during one of Jesus busy ministry campaigns that Jesus began to reveal the true secrets of his heart; the Father's purpose for his coming. *"Jesus began to tell them that the Son of Man must suffer many terrible things and be rejected . . ."* (Mark 8:31) The Greek language Jesus spoke these words indicates that Jesus held nothing back. He openly plainly revealed all. These words are in the imperfect Greek tense showing Jesus probably repeated them more than once.[22] Interrupting, as was Peter's impulsive nature, he verbally assaults Jesus.

He jumps up, pulls Jesus aside in front of the Disciples chiding him for reorganizing the Sunday morning worship service. Jesus replies, "Peter, we are changing things a bit from here on out. To reach out to people in a bigger way, where changing the second worship service. You'll play your trumpet in the first service only. Peter, my Father wants to show his love to more people. So, sorry, It's time for another plan. Greater, bigger, and exciting things are coming. Ok, Peter?"

Peter, an American Boomer a heart, censures Jesus severely, "How dare you Jesus! Who do you think you are? You can't do that! I must play my trumpet at both services! People need to hear me play Jesus. This is about me Jesus – not you. They need me. They want me. I want me too. I am important here. Ok Jesus? You got the plan down now my lord and savior?"

Christ connects with a right hook. The knockout blow hit squarely, "PETER, GET BEHIND ME SATAN!" (Mark 8:32) "THERE'S MORE GOING ON HERE THAN JUST YOU! PETER! Peter! Peter. Peter. Peter where arrreee youuuu?" Crashing back from the blow Peter responds, "Ouch! Ouch! Ouch! Mommy, Jesus is hurting me! What was happening here?" Sort of hear Ray Barone's words on Everyone Loves Raymond when confronted by a confused unfavorable situation as he cries out, "WHAT IS HAPPENING HERE?"

Peter, self-intentioned, self-aligned, and self-guided crumbled. Words rang out, "Peter, stop trying to hang onto your own life. Lose your trumpet for my sake." Peter simply did not understand the plan. How could he? He focused on his out of tune trumpet rather than his Worship Director, Jesus. Peter's ambitious plans clothed in God-words involved Peter first and foremost. His plans weren't necessarily bad. They just excluded coming events. A future he couldn't possibly anticipate. They excluded the very person he claimed to preach and love; Jesus.

Peter's heart vested itself in his trumpet. I'm going to play my trumpet Jesus! All this while the crowd sitting on the hillside in Capernaum perhaps thought, "Yes Peter, just keep missing all those high notes." In the bright lights on the stage following the notes, Peter can't see a disengaging crowd grimacing on the hillside from his off-tune trumpet. Who plans for Jesus' betrayal, suffering, and death anyways? Peter play that trumpet! Everyone loves you. Your trumpet is amazing. Everyone loves Peter. Everyone wants Peter. I love Peter. I want Peter! Jesus, stand back, and let me try that high note again, watch, here it comes, ok, here I go! Here comes the double high C. I believe; therefore, I am!

The Cornerstone of the Church blasts the future rock of the church, "Peter, you better get behind me – Satan." Crushing! Pain, the thing we flee most, is necessary and productive. Peter, more pain is coming your way. A lot more, and it's necessary for both of us. Jesus calls the crowd to gather with his disciples. His words shocked or puzzled, *"If any of you want to be my follower, you must turn from your selfish ways, take up your cross and follow me."* (Mark 8:34) Peter, I told you to put your trumpet away! Did you know in the literal Greek, the word "selfish" come from the ancient word "trumpet?" Not really. I just made that up. But, when I read this verse, I picture that old man insisting on playing his trumpet above every other consideration in the church. That old man's attitude finds common fodder in many hearts.

Trumpet Wars

Trumpets, it may surprise you, come in a variety of shapes and sizes. The coronet, for example, is a slightly smaller version of the trumpet. It's easier to hold, and makes a very mellow sound. The bugle, is used by the military. It possesses no valves. There are slide valve trumpets, soprano bugles, flugelhorns, alto trumpets, Baroque trumpets, and German trumpets.[23] Trumpets are often classified by their key and pitch. There are Bb flat trumpets, C trumpets, G trumpets, D, Eb, E and F trumpets.[24] Each trumpet serves its own special purpose to make melody among many other different instruments. Unity and harmony directed in unison produces effective music.

Once during High School band practice at Minnehaha Academy, our first chair trumpeter added an exciting, highly skilled run to the end of measure. We all heard the run. I admired it as he hit an extremely high note. Mr. Hepburn, put down his director's baton, and looked at the first chair trumpeter. With a glare, he demanded an apology. With a shrug of his shoulders the trumpet player offered a bewildered, "I'm sorry?" Mr. Hepburn replied, "Not to me. Apologize to the composer for hijacking his composition and polluting it with your own will and intent." Later in life, that trumpeter remarked, "That marked the day I became a musician."

Jesus warned of the same. He said, "Upon this rock, I will build MY Church." Tragically, we need reminding that the Church belongs to Christ, not us. Not our denominations. Not celebrity pastors. Not our hard work. Not our will and plans for the church. Our trumpets get in the way all the time. Demanding trumpet-rights diverts us from taking up our crosses

69

and following Jesus. Insisting on our trumpet-rights is another way of saving our own lives. In brandishing our trumpets insisting on sole rights, we lose our souls in the process.

There are many trumpets in the churches these days. Last year a Zulu pastor called. He described the plight of his church in South Africa. Competing trumpets stifled that church's effectiveness. The Zulu pastor moaned, "It's as if these people lost their souls in the arguments." He described his church's plight as, "Too many drums beating and smothering each other out." The many ailments among the members of that Zulu congregation mirrors churches around the world. Jesus demanded, "If you find your life, you must lose your trumpet, and whoever loses their trumpet for my sake will find it." (Matthew 10:39 – My paraphrase)

Ponderings

1. What comes to mind in Jesus' words about losing your soul?

2. How do you hit your high note?

3. Name your trumpet wars past and present

4. When does Jesus say to you, "Get behind me Satan?" Remember, Jesus loved Peter deeply. He loves you too.

5. What high price peanuts are you buying for the monkey's these days?

-7-
Soul-Cultivation
Hitting the High Note

"God is an unutterable sigh, planted in the depths of the soul."
Jean Paul

That large mega church gathering on the hillside in Galilee, either bristled or fuddled in bewilderment of Jesus words. *"Losing your life to find it, gaining the whole world, but losing your own soul,"* perplexed more than a few that day. Peter perhaps thought, "Yep, yep, got that down, Jesus! Sure, I want to follow You Jesus! You know I'm with you. Got my trumpet right here. Me and my trumpet Jesus, we are here for you. Me and my trumpet, we will play for you or die for you, Jesus."

I'll build a big church for you Jesus. I will pastor a large staff for you Jesus. I will write lots of good books, of course for you Jesus. When I attend those Christian Book Conferences, I'll push to the front, hoping to find affirmation from my peers. Playing my trumpet! I will speak at conferences, for you too. I'll gain a huge Twitter following playing my trumpet for you. My Instagram trumpet-followers are many.

I will sell a hundred cars this year, for you. And, make a good living too. I sell that Mary Kay. Purchase a nice house. In blessing myself, I'll call myself blessed, and will bless others. I'll influence many for you. I'll wear a gold cross. I'll travel all over the world leading summits, meetings, and conferences for you. I'll do that grass roots hard cross-cultural community work; for You. I'll sing songs. I'll sit in an air-conditioned building, listen to a message tailored made to my lifestyle. Give a little, serve a little, and pray a little. Sure! Count me in! I will play my trumpet! I'll play my song of Calvinism, Fundamentalism, Reformed, Arminianism, Charismatic, Evangelicalism, Traditionalism, and all the rest. I'll write blogs for you. Will highlight me for you on my Facebook, Twitter, Snap Chat, LinkedIn. I will selfie my self's self – for you! I'll lead meetings, plan, build, and grow. I will do all these things! I'm in God. I'm all in. You can count on me. And, Jesus, ah by the way, did I mention my trumpet? "PETER, put THAT TRUMPET AWAY! You're missing the high note again. Take up your cross and follow me . . . Peter, Peter, PETER!" Jesus, speaking to his most dedicated followers, warned them of losing all in their God-pursuits. It begs a huge question, "How than does one actually prevent losing your soul?"

High Note of Self-denial

Jesus continued, ***"You must deny yourself and turn from your selfish ways."*** Some maybe continued to nod their heads in agreement that day. "Ok, yes, I can do that. I will do that. I think I can do that. Wait, but how do you do that; exactly? What do you mean, Jesus?" Does that mean, "I need to forget myself, lose sight of my own interests, and center myself upon something other than just myself? What about my needs, self-care, and loving myself?"

Jesus used the same word for "denial" when he denounces Peter declaring, *"Peter, this very night you will 'deny' me three times."* Peter's denial of Jesus was absolute, complete, and resolved. As Peter cried out before a group of people gathered around a fire on a cold night, his denouncement of Jesus was resolute. "I do not even know the man!" Deny ourselves like Peter denied Christ, and we're perhaps on the right track.

Lose My What? That was not the end of Jesus; words that day. His perplexing message continued, *"If you want you try to hang on to your life, you will lose it. But if you give up your life for my sake and for the sake of the Good News, you will save it."* (Mark 8:35). Wait, I need to lose my life? What does that mean? How does that work? Why would I want to do that, Jesus?

Jesus demanded his Twelve to put their down their trumpets, and pick their crosses instead. And, here is one of the most under grasped passages in all the Bible. Jesus asks a diagnostic question, ***"And what do you benefit if you gain the whole world but lose your own soul?"*** (Mark 8:36) Let these words sink into the context of Jesus words a bit. What was Jesus saying?

In "Bible Teaching" churches, this verse usually applies to salvation; a point and moment of decision. If you don't accept Jesus, invite him into your heart, repent of your sins, or trust him, you will lose your own soul. But, . . . Jesus didn't exactly say that here. Did he? These words also find application by those who possess less than others. "Don't acquire too much because in grasping for material things and money a lot you might lose your soul." Well, but . . . now, Jesus didn't say that either. Did he?

Jesus continues to clarify, *"Is anything worth more than your soul?"* (Mark 8:37) Jesus poses a rhetorical question. **What is, worth more than your soul?** Jesus is not completely talking about only soul-destiny here. I think, he's also talking about soul-awareness. What exactly then does it mean to lose one's soul? I always interpreted this verse in my younger days as a decision that impacted where one spent eternity if compromising the spiritual over earthly things.[25] That is not exactly within the bounds of good interpretation here. Jesus was not only dealing with an eternal perspective of one's soul. He also called to attention a more current perspective of the soul.[26] What's the condition of your soul right now. Jesus wasn't just making a case for the afterlife in this passage. He presented a clear need for examination of our souls now. Our current soul-condition this very moment.[27]

High Note of the Cross

Carry a what? I suspect Jesus next words produced instant confusion, "Peter, put down your trumpet and, *'take up your cross.'*" In the ancient world, the cross brought a singularly predominant picture to mind; suffering. Jesus, you want me to suffer? The cross was in the first century not exactly a selling point to the ancient mind;[28] especially to Greeks and Romans. Unlike much teaching in the church today, the cross was not a sanitized portrayal of images, carvings, jewelry, words, and music. To the ancient mind, the cross meant only one thing; anguish, humility, and loss. The message interpreted by the ancient world may have gone like this, "Hi everyone, come worship the God we put on a cross, crucified, and killed. You want to join with us?" That cross appealed very little.[29]

High Note of Serving Others

Messages and teaching often focus on the need of others. We've consistently taught the Good Samaritan (Luke 10) lesson from a perspective of "Who is my neighbor?" Yet, for churches in the throes congregational battles, hitting the high note of serving others suffers to find its milieu. We tend to serve ourselves in our churches more than our churches serve others.

High Note of the Soul

King David, in Psalm 42, under acute pressure hits the hit note of his soul. He cries out, *"For God alone, O my soul, wait in silence, for my hope is from him."* (ESV)

Mahatma Gandhi hit his high note too. He wrote, "When I admire the wonders of a sunset or the beauty of the moon, my soul expands in the worship of the creator."

Helen Keller was the first deaf blind person to earn a degree. Known for her many accomplishments, she wrote, "Character cannot be developed in ease and quiet. Only through experience of trial and suffering can the soul be strengthened, ambition inspired, and success achieved."

Plato's view of soul-care is a personal favorite. He taught, "Thinking: the talking of the soul with itself."

What hits the high note of your soul? Deepak Chopra aims high, "We must go beyond the constant clamor of ego, beyond the tools of logic and reason, to the still, calm place within us: the realm of the soul."

What brings on all this soul talk? The answer is in what took place beforehand. Jesus just finished explaining his upcoming suffering, rejection, and crucifixion. His fulfillment of his father's plan radically diverted from the Peter's God-plan for his life. Peter's attempted to plan God into his desires and aspirations. Peter pulled Jesus aside and began to rebuke him in verse thirty-two. The word Mark chose to describe Peter's rebuke is a strong one (Gr. *epitimao*). It is the same word he used to describe Jesus silencing demons (cf. Mark 1:25; Mark 3:12). Peter reacted with "an air of conscious superiority."[30]

Peter was rejecting the very thing, the only thing, that could bring him wholeness; the Cross. The cross represented that which Peter did not care for or want to consider. Jesus rebuke is even stronger, *"Get behind Me Satan . . ."* Ouch! What then was Jesus saying?

A soul lived and focused only on itself misses its high note. A trumpet living only to sound out its own note loses out.

Your Soul. Are you losing your soul right now? Witnessed in my own life and that of others, is a tendency to lose one's soul in doing. We are doers by nature. Busy in doing, we plow forward in activity. Pastors building their churches. Missionaries building their ministries. Biblical entrepreneurs pushing towards success. Focusing on the big instead of the significant. Focusing on success rather than influence. Focusing on stuff instead of substance. Following cultural values over personal purity.

Valuing money over service. Winning often rates above compassion when focused upon doing. Values are compromised to gain personal life. Honesty is sacrificed to get ahead in business. [31] Pride hides injury. Fear prevents discovery and healing. Self-righteousness prevents considering another's perspective above your own. Sacrificing a moment of integrity for immediacy. And, busyness – the god of this culture, totally stifles any possibility for soul-examination. A life that clutters itself with only doing suffers opportunity for soul-consideration. When me becomes the center of me, I get lost.

What does anything you are doing today matter if you are losing your own soul right now? I think many of God's "saved people" lose a bit of their souls each day. I think some of my Catholic friends striving to become good Catholics lose their own souls while compartmentalizing faith and life. Many striving for righteous causes perhaps lose themselves in good things. Miniature idols erect themselves over their soul's landscapes of life. What we do, fear, hide, or highly value perhaps unknowingly become the gods we worship. In doing life and ministry my saved soul got lost.

For me, trauma so wounded my soul, that a personal examination of my soul's condition changed my life. It's here that I regained my soul.

High Note of Soul-examination

Examination is the emphasis of Jesus words here. Jesus, speaking mainly to his disciples just denounced Peter. "Get away from me, Satan!" Now, let's think about Christ's words for a moment. Was Jesus saying, "Peter, if you're not careful you will lose your soul and spend forever in hell?" Jesus didn't say that. Jesus clarified, *"For you are not setting your mind on God's interests, but man's."* (NASB) Jesus pressed Peter, "Where is God in your plans Peter?"

High Note of Soul-Value

What's Worth More Than My Soul? Don, nothing wrong with that new Kia Sorento, but it's not worth more than your soul. Don, God allowed you to do some great ministry in South Africa. You built some great buildings and a good organization. Good for you! But, make sure you're hitting the right note. You helped a lot of sick dying children. Good for you. Are you hitting the right high note too?

Lose your own soul. Hum, trying to hang onto life while losing it. Hanging onto a career, paying countless sacrifices to succeed, yet, losing a soul in the process. Hanging onto a relationship, only to lose one's self in the process. Hanging onto expectations, a better place in life, asking yourself, "How did I get here? Is this all? Is there nothing better?" A staggering loss, and a wandering searches soul looking for reason. A nice house, SUV, boat, cabin, another vehicle, but . . . the soul?

Doing a lot god-stuff in the church. Elder, deacon, pastor, missionary, teacher, or attender and yet losing one's soul. Performing on the church stage before a large audience as fog floats across the stage, music cranked, lights cascading in every direction and color – is it possible to lose one's soul? Preparing and delivering a thousand Bible messages while losing one's soul in the process?

Obsessed with acquiring life, hoarding it, clinging to it, defending it, and striding to gain more, many arrive at an empty cul-de-sac. They miss the very thing they sought. Jesus words challenge a practical examination of our soul's condition. What exactly am I living for? What's my soul-condition? What's going on in my soul right this moment?

Years of grappling with the crushing traumatic deaths of so many children in our feeding centers in South Africa witnessed – my development of my own lostness. Standing in front of a casket with a parent in Northern Minnesota with a widow whose husband dropped dead two years' prior now looking at her daughter's body in a casket killed by a drunk driver - lostness. A paper mill closing, laying off workers five years from retirement - lostness.

As Chaplain of the Grand Rapids, Minnesota Fire Department in Northern Minnesota, sitting with a mother in the ER, her eight-year-old son lay motionless before her. His body robbed of life trying to save his little sister from drowning. He succeeded in saving his sister, but lost his little life in the heroic effort. Lostness.

A pastor just this week shared his story of he and his wife trying to pastor a sizable church. In a busy ministry, they struggle to raise their grandchildren in their advancing years. He described his battle with depression. Looking at me tenderly he signed, *"Sometimes my soul gets so weary."* The ancient man Job in the Old Testament resonates, *"My soul is weary of my life . . ."* Job 10:1 (KJV)

As Lon cried out that Christmas Eve, "My soul is in a haze" his cluttered words repeated themselves uttered by discouraged pastors, missionaries, church members, friends, and family. Soul-haze surrounds many faith-followers. Maybe Lon's words were soul words. A cry uttering, "I lost my soul. Where did it go?"

PONDERINGS

1. What is the condition of your soul?

2. How might you describe your soul? Hard question?

3. Why don't we spend more time talking about the now condition of our souls?

4. How can you better care for your soul? The real you.

5. Do you suffer from soul-haze? How would you describe it?

6. What do you think Jesus meant when he said, *"And what do you benefit if you gain the whole world but lose your own soul?*

7. Jesus also said, *"Is anything worth more than your soul?"* What do these words speak to you?

8. What does the term soul-care mean to you?

-8-
Soul-Health
Clearing the Weeds

"You do realize that you are a termite.
You are eating through my soul."[32]
Mary Amato, Guitar Notes

"Dear friends, I warn you as 'temporary residents and foreigners' to
keep away from worldly desires that
wage war against your very souls."
Apostle Peter, 1 Epistle of Peter

Hitting the high note in a soul requires clearing out contaminants hindering health. I dislike gardening. My oldest son, Donnie, on the other hand lives and breathes plants, vegetables, fruit trees, and bees. Twice a week, he's in his garden teaching his children how to weed, care for fruit trees, and take care of his honey producing bees. Just today, he posted on his Facebook our grandchildren holding huge radishes pulled from their garden. I'd like to say he got his horticultural leanings from me. He did not.

Once, and only once, I attempted a garden when our sons were young. Thinking it a great family project, tons of work went into breaking soil, tilling soil, establishing a few garden beds, erecting a fence, and then planting corn, beans, lettuce, radishes, and potatoes. Why anyone plants radishes is beyond me. Within ten days, shoots emerged from the soil. After another ten days, unwanted companions joined our green little friends. After a few weeks, life got busy, and we sort of forgot about the garden. The family project turned into a place of avoidance as the weeds grew thick and fast. After a first initial harvest of a few heads of lettuce and beans, gardening techniques changed. The following year's gardening season found me standing in the aisles of the local grocery between the fruit and vegetable stands. Quite enjoyed gardening from then on as we never suffered another problem with weeds in our garden beds.

Once word came about one our water sources at a rural church outside of Ladysmith. In St. Chad's, our little church also cared for about twenty Zulu orphan children. Simon, as he wished to be called since most English speakers couldn't pronounce his Zulu name; Umdlandlankulu, directed the Orphan Center. He reported the children all suffered from stomach problems and diarrhea. A water test performed indicated the water high in bacteria. The cause; numerous outhouses throughout the community were seeping into the ground polluting the drinking water sourced at the local well. The water was contaminated. The entire community fell ill. With help from Rotary International a new deeper well provided the community with clean drinking water.

Growing up in the Catholic Church, my understanding of Soul Contaminants revolved around committing sins. In Catholicism, one commits venial or mortal sins. Venial sins got you in trouble, mortal sins sent you to hell. Apart from confession, penitence, and absolution a person stood in great trouble. There was a whole list of venial sins set before us during my Confirmation classes. Talking back to your parents, stealing, grumbling, eating fish on Friday's, going to unapproved movies, and considerable other little vices made up a list of No-no's to steer clear from. As a young kid, Mortal Sins were not within personal leanings, but the venial sins troubled me a lot.

In 1973 when "saved" entered my vocabulary, the Baptist Naughty No-No's marked acres of intruders needing constant weeding from one's life. It was rather exhausting trying to identify, remove, or stay away from all those pests. No movies, no pants on women, no cussing, no missing church, no long hair on men, and as Sonny and Cher used to sing, "The beat goes on."

A Church of the Nazarene friend of mine once commented as I shared this story, "Oh, yah, we had those too! We called them the Nazarene "No-no's." Their No-no's resembled verbatim, most the No-no's in our Baptist Churches at the time. The biggest No-no all held in common was, "Thou shalt not attend any other church, but our church."

These No-no's typically focused upon the social ills of the day. In 1973 upon "accepting Christ" No-no's went like this. Thou shalt not drink. Thou shalt not go to movies. All movies are bad. Thou shalt not listen to unchristian music. The Who, Eagles, Beatles, and John Denver for that matter, were all out. I soon learned the definition of Christian music. Christian music is whatever they liked, and I did not. Thou shalt not dress like this or that. Thou shalt not, not, not, not . . . The "Not" family, I soon learned, was the largest most influential family in the church.

Looking back, all those No-no's didn't really seem to help anyone. Forbidding simply encouraged adventure. And, it sentenced rule violators to live in guilt, shame, and fear. No-no's seemed to put people into more bondage; not less. However, the No-no's did accomplish one thing exceptionally well. For those who followed the No-no's Rule Book, it created a self-righteous, looking down your nose, judgmental closed-mined exclusive group of people in the church. Usually, they ran the church.

Door County, Wisconsin is a favorite tourist destination. The protruding peninsula separating Green Bay and Lake Michigan accounts for its name.[33] The narrow "Door" presents varieties of recreational activities, scenery, nature, and wildlife. Often, we've driven the entire peninsula stopping at a variety of coffee and antique shops. It's simply breath taking at times.

In 2007, after eating, 229 people were sickened at a local restaurant. Seven more were hospitalized by the Norovirus. Usually known for attacking mainly cruise ship goers. The cause of the near epidemic was a leaking septic system close to the restaurant's establishment contaminating their well.[34] The thought of a leaking septic tank and eating meals tainted from human feces paints a grim picture. Those patrons literally consumed micro remains of their own, and others, human fecal matter.

The often-impulsive Peter, who fumbled and bumbled in his earlier years with both feet in his mouth, brings strong warning. Years later, maturing in faith and person, while living under persecution, he urges followers to guard their souls. He lists certain contaminants. His comments in his letter to persecuted Christians throughout the ancient world is puzzling. In the throes of Christians being martyred at seemingly every turn, he insisted soul-care a most essential personal concentration. Soul-care over self-preservation and survival? Really?

His language is strong using the term, "war." He exclaims *"I urge you as aliens and strangers to abstain from fleshly lusts which wage war against the soul."* 1 Peter 2:11 (NASB) The terms "aliens" and "strangers" gives evidence to the quality of life followers of Jesus endured. They were at war, but the war was for possession of their souls rather than the Roman government. Peter warns followers to protect their souls. This was their top priority. When is the last time you ever thought, "How will I protect my soul today?"

The picture of "war" here is that of a commander leading a band of soldiers on military ops into the deepest place of one's person.[35] These enemies Peter calls, "fleshly lusts." Making incursions into the soul, fleshly lusts wreak havoc. "Fleshly lusts" is literally thinking and acting in merely animalistic instincts and cravings.[36] Sometimes it's simply translated, "desires." It's these desires, Peter warns cast the soul into a haze of weakness and ultimately destruction.

A closer study of "abstain" discovers this word used by Peter is the Greek word "Apotithemi." "In the language Peter wrote, it literally refers to the laying aside of one's garments or removing a robe. Figuratively apotithemi meant to cease doing what one was accustomed to doing. Stop doing it, 'throw it off' and be done with it."[37] He lists a number of soul sickening contaminants. These made up Peter's No-no's in 1 Peter 2:1.

UPROOT MALICE

In fourth grade many years ago, some educator or school committee thought dance classes a great addition to the Physical Education curriculum. So, there we were in that old little gym at Lowell Elementary School in North Minneapolis circa 1968. Before us stood our heavy-set aging fifth grade teacher Mrs. M instructing us on the art and value of square dancing. This is in Minneapolis mind you. Not somewhere out in West Kansas. Adding to our embarrassment and discomfort was Mrs. M's attempt to demonstrate some square-dancing moves with the unfortunate boy that day in gym. Poor Calvin! After the dance moves, I knew I'd need psychiatric care the rest of my life. Still see portly Mrs. M. in that bright yellow dress with blue sun bursts calling out dosidos. It looked a little more like a WWE Match than any dancing I'd ever seen.

Then she divided the children into two groups. The boys in one line facing stood facing the girls in another line ten feet apart. Here's where my prayer life discovered fervency. In the girl's line stood Doris. No one liked nor wanted to dance with her. Doris was the most undesirable girl in the whole school. Why, I don't know. There was nothing wrong with Doris. She wasn't a horrible little person. Her only shortcoming was in her appearance. Coming from a very poor home, she dressed unacceptably. Her clothes appeared tattered and ragged. Often her hair was unkempt. Usually, she arrived at school with her face unwashed. Added to this, was her sullen dejected look encompassed by a rather homely looking demeanor. Doris was our undesirable. She existed at the bottom of our pecking order. And, peck we did. Malice and

89

bullying presented itself, even in those early years in that fourth-grade dance class among those thirty-twelve-year old's.

As our teacher began to pair up each boy and girl, boys began to comment, "I hope I don't get ugly Doris. Some of the girls called out, "Who's going to get ugly Doris?" Those malicious comments hit their mark recurrently as Doris evidenced emotional pain grimacing and wincing with each comment. Her pain showed in her wounded eyes. A look she directed at me as the number of possible partners diminished.

I prayed in my heart, "God, please, please, please, PLEASE not Doris, please not Doris God, God, please, please, please . . ." Then experiencing the disappointment of unanswered prayer, the teacher called out, "Don and Doris!" The reaction on my face communicated my message, "Doris, I don't want you, I don't want this. You're not wanted or desired. Ugh, no, not YOU! Doris!" Added to both our embarrassment was a barrage of ugly little comments coming from the already paired couples, "Don got ugly Doris." It was ugly alright, but the hideousness of that morning laid not to with Doris, but with us.

Malice wounded a lot of souls that day; ours, mine, and especially Doris'. I've often thought about Doris over the years. One might say, "Well, you were only children. It wasn't that big a deal. You committed only a venial sin." Hum, or was it a mortal sin? I wonder? How might Doris respond? Sure, we were kids. We were young. No one got hurt; maybe, honestly, not really. Self-inflicted harm fell upon us all that morning. Ill will, vindictiveness, and maleficence began in small kindling hearts.

In a court of law, malice is often examined to discover "wrongful intention" and determine the level of guilt of a specific crime against a person.[38] Black's Law Dictionary provides a helpful understanding of the depth and intent of "malice."

> In its legal sense, this word does not simply mean ill will against a person, but signifies a wrongful act done intentionally, without just cause or excuse. A conscious violation of the law (or the prompting of the mind to commit it) which operates to the **prejudice of another person.** About as clear, comprehensive, and correct a definition as the afford is that "malice is a condition of the mind which shows a heart regardless of social duty and fatally bent on mischief, the existence of which is inferred from acts committed or words spoken. "Malice," in its common acceptation, means ill will towards some person.[39] (Bold Face Mine)

Many lawsuits are won or lost based on whether malicious intent is proven. If a prosecutor can prove intent to do harm, a claim of innocence is in great doubt. Malice or lack thereof can determine the fate of the defendant.

Hurting another person is often well bedded in thought and action by age twelve. The average age to join a gang in the United States is between 14-16 years of age. It is during adolescence, kids belonging to gangs maliciously injure communities throughout the United States.[40] Malice begins small and metastasizes into ominous effect.

I wish perhaps to meet Doris again. I've often thought about her over the years. Wonder if she went to college, married, had kids, and enjoyed some sense of happiness in life. I've thought of what words I might use to reassure Doris of her value to God and me. How a request for forgiveness might be attempted. Not just for myself, but for the entire fourth grade class that day in gym. That old school and neighborhood are gone now, but Doris still lives on in my mind.

Watching the news outlets and media also draws conclusions about intent. It appears the News isn't so much about reporting news any longer. News reporting seeks more to discredit than report. Least that's the way it looks to me. Politicians join these ranks too. No longer is debate about policy and issues. It seeks to paint the bleakest picture of the other candidate's character, integrity, and person. Politics is no longer about America. It's about malice, inflicting the highest damage on the opponent's character to win elections. Malice. Our country is rife with it from the highest level down to our streets. Trickle down maleficence affects us. It's our nature. To hurt one another. We do it often, we do it well, and we are lethal. It kills our souls, wounds our persons, and lessons us as a people.

Maleficence chokes our soul's goodness. Malice is an enemy destroying the good stuff in our soul's garden. Left unattended, these invaders take over the soul. The bitter nasty crud crowds out love, goodness, and joy. Our souls become beds of thorns and briers. Painful to touch or draw close to. A lethal toxin.

Peter strongly warns us, "**To put these things off.**" In some translations, the word "abstain" is used. Abstain from these contaminants. The idea here is to "hold one's self off."[41] We are to hold ourselves off from allowing ill-will to gain a foothold in our souls. Every fight I've ever witnessed in the church between "members" carried ample measures of malice imbedded into the hearts of the "righteous" seeking to defeat the other side over an issue.

Once an elder at the church I served as pastor sought to discredit every person the board. In the congregation were many members who worked for this elder. Those members claimed the leader was stealing their retirement money from their 401k retirement plans. As the elder claimed to be "kind," he accused each of a sundry of deficiencies. It divided people. That elder a year later was sentenced to a prison term for embezzlement and theft of his employee's retirement funds and benefits. "Kind" proved malice. Though never admitted, that elder went to prison justified in his mind that he, not his employees, was the real victim. Numerous families lost their entire retirement savings. Maliciousness worked with devastating effect as families in the community lost their homes.

UPROOT DECEIT

Deceit is another enemy that wars against one's soul. Peter warns, *"Rid yourself of all malice and all deceit."* (NIV) Two qualities stand out here. First, the removal process, "rid." The idea is to clear or remove as in taking off a coat or robe. Next is the extent of the removal; absolute, complete. These soul-contaminants require complete removal down to the very last trace. Weeding one's soul-bed is not about controlling these contaminants. It's about eliminating each inclination; COMPLETELY.

One of the members of a church I pastored offered to take me duck hunting. Desiring to get to know that member better, I agreed. Meeting in the early morning darkness, along with his son, we made our way to "his favorite place" pulling his duck boat behind. Launching the boat with the three of us along with his dog, dozens of decoys, and other sundry items we reached a patch of high cattails and reeds fifty yards off shore. The first hour was spent placing decoy after decoy in meticulous order on the water. The decoys had to look lifelike in the hope of attracting ducks. And, attract them they did.

The first wave of ducks flew in shortly after sunrise. With great precision, the father and his son brought down several ducks. With a command, the dog alighted from the boat and retrieved each duck. First wave dad and son 3 – pastor Don 0. The next wave approached after thirty minutes. As they landed just in front of our duck boat, blind shots rang out. After the second round the score stood, dad and son 7 ducks – pastor Don 1 decoy.

Yep, amid the Mallards, Red Heads, Teals, and a host of other winged fowls I ended up shooting a rather expensive decoy. With all the commotion, personal confusion reigned as I couldn't tell the difference between ducks landing in the water and the decoys next to them. Ducks fled the pellet filled air flying from our boat. One decoy stood out from the others. It lay on its side in a new, unusual configuration filled with buckshot.

At the end of the morning towards noon, about a dozen ducks lay in our boat, and one obliterated decoy. Later that evening after preparing the fowls, wrapping them in bacon, and cooking them, we sat down to a duck banquet with many other friends. Stories abounded about the day's hunting exploits while trying to consume cooked duck that embarrassing night. Quickly, I discovered the only part of a cooked duck worth eating is the wrapped bacon. Better to leave the ducks be. Their beauty came from looking at them, not eating them. Went back to fishing from a boat after that.

When Peter used the word "deceit" this is in part, perhaps what he had in mind; decoys. The Greek word he used is "dolos" and probably comes from a very ancient word "delo" meaning to decoy.[42] Deceitfulness carries the idea of acting stealthily in craftiness and guile. It particularly refers to treacherous behavior.

"Guile" is sometimes used in place of "deceit." Both words carry the idea to decoy or to bait. Literally it refers to a fishhook, trap, or trick all of which represent various forms of deception. Raised in Northern Minnesota, fishing was and still is a favorite hobby. The greater skill at baiting a hook, the greater chance of catching fish. Good fishermen show great skills at deception. Making a piece of metal or plastic dangling before some fish look like a worm, minnow, or leach requires skill and aptitude in trickery. Fishermen are skilled at deception. Likewise, some show equally skilled abilities at outright lying as they recount the "big one" that got away!

Dolos is a deliberate attempt to mislead, trick, snare or bait. Baiting a trap to "catch" an unwary victim through deception. It is a desire to gain an advantage. To get the better of another through cunningness.

A modern term in advertising is called "bait and switch." This is a tactic used by advertisers where an unwary consumer is lured in by what looks like a price too good to be true![43] 80% off was a sign I saw the other day in a local store. The discounted price was $19.99. People took the bait buying the item. Some quick math brought an interesting conclusion. If the item was truly discounted by 80%, it meant the item was normally priced at $100.00. This proved clearly deceptive. The price for the item was never $100.00. No one would purchase it at that price. Once I saw a sign displaying, "110% off." So, I asked, "Does that mean if I take this, you'll GIVE me 10 cents back for every dollar on this item?" The store employee chuckled.

Deceit is particularly toxic. Not only to the deceptive soul, but to those it deceives. In its basest form, deceit is deception with words. When attempted flattery, false promises, false tales, suggestive talk, off-colored suggestions, or enticing words dishonesty occurs. Deceit or guile simply means to outright lie with the intent to decoy.[44]

UPROOT HYPOCRICSY

Peter adds a third element onto his list of soul toxins; hypocrisy. Hypocrisy is a word much bandied about these days. Heard it ad nauseam as a pastor. "I don't go to the church because of all those hypocrites!" Referring often to someone two-faced or inconsistent in words and deeds, it falls short of its origin.

Hypocrite comes from two words describing one who acts pretentiously, a counterfeit, and a person who acts under a feigned character. A hypocrite is someone who pretends to be something he or she is not. It refers literally to delivery of a speech, along with interpretive gestures and imitation. Hypocrisy involves the art of mask-wearing.[45]

The word hypocrisy comes from ancient Greek theater and referred to the practice of putting on a mask and playing a part on stage. By wearing a mask, an actor could project a character. That character projected was not the actual person behind the mask. There was the real person and the unreal projected person. Hypocrisy is the practice of projecting a disingenuous person; a fake.

Hypocrisy in the New Testament carries only negative connotations. Referring to duplicity, it implies the quality belying one's true intentions by deceptive words or action. Insincerity, dissimulation, or hiding under false pretense is the idea here. Disguising one's thoughts or feelings for deceptive motives is a contaminant we all display from time to time.

The idea is to pretend, to act as something one is not. It creates an impression that is at odds with one's real purposes or motivations. Hypocrisy is characterized by play-acting, pretense, or outward show. It means to give an impression of having certain purposes or motivations, while having quite different ones, usually to the harm of another individual.[46]

UPROOT ENVY

In Ezakheni, South Africa, there lived a rather successful wealthy Zulu man. From his home, he ran his personal taxi business. Behind the fences of his home stood eleven vans much to the envy of many. Every morning his drivers showed up, picked up a set of keys to a van, and began collecting passengers ferrying them back and forth to town for the next twelve hours. In the evening when the drivers returned, the vans were parked, keys handed in, and the gates locked. The disdain and envy his success produced in his younger brothers grew renown throughout the area. Repeatedly, his brothers shared their desire to partner with the older brother in his business endeavors. The older brother repeatedly refused. Often, voicing their concerns to the older brother in front of his home produced quite the spectacle. Arguing, yelling, and conflict between the brothers over the course of several years secured a name by the community. The place became known in Zulu as, "The House Where Brothers Fight."

One morning, drivers arrived at the home to begin their routes. Upon arrival, gates were open, and not a single van remained. A quick inspection of the home found the older brother shot to death. Within the week the younger brothers were rounded up and charged with murder. The younger brothers' malice gained footholds in their hearts until their fleshly desires metastasized. Acting upon evil thoughts, murdered ensued. Envy ruled. Ruined lives followed.

UPROOT SLANDER

A once well-known pastor in the 19th century told a story to explain "slander." He said, "There is a little mischief in the village about Miss A or Mr. B, and Mrs. Tittle-tattle is up as early as possible, and calls on Mrs. Scandal, and says, 'Have you heard the sad news? I hope it is not true.' 'No, I have not heard it.' 'Well, don't mention it to anybody else. I hope it is not correct, but I have heard so-and-so.' And the two sit down, and they make such a breakfast over it. And they both say they hope it is not true, while all the time they are as glad of it in their hearts as ever they can be. They go on telling others they hope it is not true, and telling them not to mention it to anybody else, until they do all the mischief before they have stopped to inquire whether they are telling lies." (Spurgeon, UBS Handbook)[47]

Slander at its most extreme form is to speak in untrue worse terms of another to destroy their credibility and person. The word of choice to describe this attribute is defamation. We are easily lured into self-thinking that such a quality is beyond us. A closer study of "slander" shows a leaning culpability present in most of us.

"Slander" comes from the Greek word, "katalalia" and means "speaking against" or "speaking down" to a person describing the act of defaming or slandering.[48] It is to shoot someone down with words.[49] Using words, slander causes maximum damage to a person's character tainting an individual to the lowest possible extreme. It is to destroy a person through words.

Slander is perhaps the sin of choice more common in the church. Last week a pastor called asking for advice. He described a situation of a couple in his church. Both husband and wife grew up in the church. Their parents and grandparents were also members. For some reason, beyond his ability to ascertain, this couple went to each small group in the church charging the pastor with "Spiritual Abuse." The wife attended each woman's gathering. There she leveled the charge, "This pastor is, "Spiritually Abusive." The husband attended, in most cases for the first time, every men's event. Sitting among twenty men during Bible Study, he asked to share a prayer request. It went like this. "Please pray for our pastor as many of us are concerned he's over stepping his authority." This pastor was the last to find out about all of this.

Upon his last church meeting before his resignation, he sat with two elders and the couple. When asked about the charges, both husband and wife failed to produce a single instance of Spiritual Abuse – whatever the nebulous abstract phrase means. What they did decry was their soon replacement as directors of youth after THEY resigned six months prior. The new couple taking their place to lead the youth were far more qualified and talented. The decision to replace the quitting couple was in fact initiated by the elders, not that pastor. Those elders said nothing.

Within six months, that Senior Pastor was gone. So, too the talented new Youth Director husband and wife. Slandered they also left. The Executive Pastor followed a few months later. And, today, that slanderous couple once again "leads the youth." A position they were not trained for nor particularly gifted to perform. And, church attendance is now half of what it was. Slander through this couple shot its many arrows piercing souls to ruin.

While recently visiting a church, a large man approached. The voice inside said, "Watch out this guy is up to no good." Having spoken at this large church a few times over the years, guess he figured he "knew" me. As a captive in the church's coffee shop he began shooting arrows of slander at the pastor, senior leadership, and church. He used words like, "Dishonest, money hungry, nepotism, and cover up." I stopped him abruptly and asked him if he'd spoken to any of the people named about the things he said. He answered, "No." That week, much to his dislike, I informed the senior staff of his complaints suggesting they make a call and invite him in for a conversation. They followed my advice, and slander held its tongue. At least for a while.

A perfect example of slander is found in Genesis 39. Joseph was a captive slave serving in the house of a wealthy Egyptian named Potiphar. Apparently, Joseph was quite an attractive young man as Potiphar's wife made sexual advances towards him. Joseph repeatedly refused her advances. When she couldn't seduce the young man, she slandered Joseph accusing him of attempted rape. For that Joseph went to solitary confinement in an Egyptian prison. He spent years there because of a handful of lies. Potiphar's wife willfully spoke falsely about Joseph with the intent of damaging his reputation.

James, the half-brother of Jesus used a reasoning approach to warn against the dangers of slander. He wrote to Jewish Christians, *"Don't speak evil **(defame)** against each other, dear brothers and sisters. If you criticize and judge each other, then you are criticizing and judging God's law. But your job is to obey the law, not to judge whether it applies to you. God alone, who gave the law, is the Judge. He alone has the power to save or to destroy. So what right do you have to judge your neighbor?"* (James 4:11-12 – Bold Face mine) James encouraged us to spend our energy obeying the law rather than defaming others by it.

The Great Fire of Rome started July 18th, 64 A.D. Huge swaths of the ancient city were destroyed. Many citizens of Rome believed their Caesar, Nero, responsible for the fire. Nero chose to make Christians scapegoats. Thousands were rounded up, tortured, and murdered in the most brutal of ways. Peter's writings mention little of this. His emphasis focused not on a temporal Rome, but on a person's immortal the soul.

"So clean house! Make a clean sweep of malice and pretense, envy and hurtful talk. You've had a taste of God. Now, like infants at the breast, drink deep of God's pure kindness. Then you'll grow up mature and whole in God. Friends, this world is not your home, so don't make yourselves cozy in it. Don't indulge your ego at the expense of your soul." (1 Peter 2:1-3;11 The Message)

Ponderings

1. How healthy is your soul?

2. What weeds grow in your soul-garden?

3. What contaminants seek to sicken and damage your soul?

4. How can you cultivate your soul towards better health?

5. What needs uprooting from your life?

-9-
Soul-Affliction
Making Sense Out of Suffering

Maybe it's due to personal suffering during childhood. Or, perhaps twenty years of living among suffering Zulu people in South Africa Or, watching countless Zulu children die before their helpless mothers. Leaving for the United States, Africa accompanied me in a suitcase named PTSD. Making sense out of suffering centers much of my thinking.

Once in the U.S, scores of mentally anguished parishioners coming to their pastor for help asked repeatedly, "Why?" With the traumatic loss of a foster child, we asked, "Why?" Yesterday, a crying woman I barely knew called me. Speaking at the church she attended six months ago, she reached out. Her daughter overdosed on alcohol and opioids last week, she begged, "Would you please do my daughters funeral?" Then she asked, "Why?" It's a painful question asked of me many times over the years. As if, I possess the answers to such tragedies.

Much of my training is in "Christ-Centered Biblical Counseling." This model of counseling points us towards God's purposes in suffering.[50] In Christ, suffering finds a greater purpose. However, connecting the dots from truth to experience is daunting at times. Biblical counselors understand that not all suffering is a direct result of personal sin, but rather the result of living in a fallen and depraved world.[51] Christ-

Centered Biblical Counseling seeks to identify suffering with the Great Sufferer; Jesus on the Cross. Rather than a passive victim because of what others have done to me, or the way I'm being treated today, God's Word through Jesus Christ drives us to better conclusions.[52] While my theological mind agreed with much of my training, PTSD and experience often occurred far distanced from practical help or application. Experience and theology struggled to find common ground of companionship at times. During some very dark days, I looked to the Cross again.

Sitting in churches over the years looking at crosses, hearing messages on The Cross, and listening to music about the Cross, it appears sterile and clinical at times. The old song says, "Love grew where the blood fell . . ." One of my personal favorites in the day. Another favorite is Chris Tomlin's "Where Your love ran red and my sin washed white, I owe all to You, I owe all to You, Jesus." Or, "Lead me to the cross." Great songs, but that horrible, wonderful day when Christ hung in traumatic misery, stands in stark contrast to crosses hanging in many churches today. Colored lighting illuminating crosses hanging in churches present an opposite view of that day on Golgotha – The Place of the Skull.

Raised in Catholicism at St. Phillips and St. Ann's Church in North Minneapolis, Christ was presented as a suffering Savior. Crucifixes pictured Christ hanging on the cross in trauma and torment. Evangelical and Fundamental Christianity cries, "Christ is not on the cross any longer. He is risen, and the cross is empty." Yes, true. Yet, for millions if not billions, daily life identifies more with the Suffering Christ on the Cross than Resurrected Christ in Heaven. For many, life hangs on a cross of suffering next to Jesus awaiting the words, *"I assure you, today you will be with me in paradise."* Peter Rollings' states this well:

> On the cross Christ is rejected by his friends, betrayed by the religious authorities and crucified by the political leaders. We witness here, in the starkest of terms, the loss of all those structures that ground us and give us the sense that life makes sense (the religious, cultural and political). More than this Christ experiences the loss of that which grounds each of these realms ("My God, My God, why have you forsaken me"). [53]

During all those years by the bedsides of dying Zulus in South Africa, Christ hung on that cross. At crash scenes extricating the wounded out of crumpled cars, the suffering Christ was nearby. With the sick and suffering – the Crucifix with a suffering Christ upon it gives identity and comfort. And, on that day, as a six-year-old standing behind the curtain hiding while my five-year-old brother received a beating of a galley slave, the Suffering Christ was nearby.

On that Cross, the Savior hung in anguish those last few hours of his earthly life. Those moments find identity with the human experience today.

I like Peter Rollins' caution that a surface view of the cross advocates "nothing more than a Roller-Coaster version of Christianity – a voyeuristic sense of danger robbed of its trauma."[54] Making sense out of our personal suffering, may I humbly point you to that desolate old cross Jesus hung on before a few weeping friends, a jeering crowd, and mocking Roman military?

In St. Joseph's Church in Grand Rapids, Minnesota a bronze replica of Jesus on the Cross hangs from a cross. With one hand and feet nailed to the cross, Christ's right hand is free reaching up in agony to his Father.[55] During my chaplaincy and fire department duties from funerals to 911 Memorial services, it is the Christ I most identified with in suffering. Wreathing in pain, the Son accomplishing his Father's will reaches heavenward to set people free.

Someone Who Understands

Ten years of sleepless nights, aversion to noise, night sweats, chronic pain, hopelessness, mood swings, light aversion, and fear to share this stuff with anyone brought me to focus on the crucified Christ. Considering his unjust treatment, misunderstood intentions, betrayals, attacks, accusations, scourging, and hideous death, brought him closer to me than ever before. ***"Since he himself has gone through suffering and testing, he is able to help us . . ."*** (Hebrews 2:18), Christ is right there with us in our suffering. Jesus' soul experienced deep grief. (Matthew 26:38). As he reached out to his disciples for sympathy and companionship during the lonely hours in the Garden, his friends let him down. Jesus understands deep disappointment.

During many painful hours tracing back the sources of my PTSD, it was as if Christ said to me, "I understand Don; I've been here before too. I know about mental anguish; dysfunctional relationship, family problems, physical abuse, pain, and suffering. You have a helper to get you through this." (John 14:16)

Someone Who Gives Purpose

One very surprising aspect of my suffering was that it caused Christ to suffer too. Scripture teaches that Christ carried my pain and anguish.

> Yet it was our weaknesses he carried; it was our sorrows that weighed him down. And we thought his troubles were a punishment from God, a punishment for his own sins! But he was pierced for our rebellion, crushed for our sins. He was beaten so we could be whole. He was whipped so we could be healed. All of us, like sheep, have strayed away. We have left God's paths to follow our own. Yet the Lord laid on him the sins of us all. (Isaiah 53:4-6)

Wow! That gives suffering a little different perspective. Doesn't it? Christ carried those unfortunate, painful events during my childhood. It was *"our sorrows that weighed him down."* My sorrows weighed Christ down. Note the next part of that verse, ***"We thought his troubles were a punishment from God . . ."*** Don't know how many times I've heard, "What have I done to deserve this?" Many Africans believe their suffering a direct result of their ancestor's displeasure with their actions. Americans often asked, "Why me?"

Making You Better

John C. Maxwell in his book, *Intentional Living: Choosing a Life the Matters,* sites a famous study by Victor and Mildred Goertzel of how adversity shaped influential people. In the book, *Cradles of Eminence,* the home backgrounds of three hundred highly successful people were studied. The list included Franklin D. Roosevelt, Helen Keller, Winston

Churchill, Albert Schweitzer, Clara Barton, Gandhi, Albert Einstein, and Sigmund Freud. The results all showed an incredible path of suffering:

- Three-fourths grew up in poverty, broken homes, or dysfunctional families
- Seventy-four of the eighty-five writers and poets came from psychologically challenging upbringings
- Over one-fourth suffered severe physical handicaps.[56]

Paul discovered long ago, suffering can help develop, strengthen, and build confidence. Why? God's love is revealed through his suffering Son and Holy Spirit.

> We can rejoice, too, when we run into problems and trials, for we know that they help us **develop** endurance. And endurance **develops** strength of character, and character **strengthens** our **confident** hope of salvation. And this hope will not lead to disappointment. For we know how dearly God loves us, because he has given us the Holy Spirit to fill our hearts with his love. (Romans 5:3-5)

Lens of Understanding

Sitting on the other side of my PTSD diagnoses, my soul lives healthier today than ever. Three women helped me see God's purpose in such suffering. One woman, a professional life and executive coach asked me this question, **"Don, do you see the tremendous <u>gift</u> God has given you?"** Her words reverberated the exact same question from another friend – a family therapist, **"Don, can you see the gift here?"** My initial thoughts were, "What are you stupid?" Only PTSD suffers understand the Valley of the Shadow of Death PTSD drags one through in agony. The third woman is my sweet wife. Through it all, Kathy came to also see purpose in my suffering. In our suffering. As we suffered together, we sold our home and began a new ministry to reach out to other missionaries and 3rd world pastors struggling to see purpose in suffering.

Suffering – A Gift

Once a very quiet man asked to talk with his pastor. Sitting in my office, tears welled in the bearded man's eyes as he spoke softly, "My son was shot and killed. It was an accident. The boys were out hunting behind our home in the woods. My oldest son followed behind my younger son." I thought, "When was this?" Pausing and looking down he struggled. His words fell to the floor, "Somehow, the gun went off. We think the safety was off. Walking through heavy brush, the gun went off. His brother dropped right in front of him. We called 911, but being so far out in the country, my son died before they could get to us." For over an hour the man broken in soul, cried out adding, "And, my other son isn't doing very well with it all. He's been to doctors and psychiatrists, but nothing helps." As the conversation continued, it centered upon his wife.

Every Sunday after second service, I reached out to a thin, barely able to stand mentally frail woman. Unable to talk, there was never conversation. The man in my office continued, "My wife used to be an athlete; very active. She played in softball and volleyball leagues. But now, well after our son's death . . . she's just what she is now." Then a most alarming fact slipped out. "Ever since my son died **twenty years ago** she's never been the same." I thought, "Twenty-years!? This poor family has suffered like this for twenty years?" What Sunday Morning Cross messages or Cross teachings could possibly offer comfort to such a traumatized family? What can one say? What might I say to help? I just listened hurting in my soul with him.

Composing himself he continued, "We don't talk about it much anymore. People don't want to hear about it. It makes them uncomfortable. Guess that's why we have no friends anymore." I listened quietly, then looking at me he probed, "Have you ever held a dying child before?" My quite answer surprised him, "Yes, unfortunately too many times." He challenged me, "Oh, really, tell me." After our conversation finished that morning he left my office with a lumberjack's handshake commenting, "Thanks, pastor. This really helped me this morning." As I smiled, I thought, "Really, really?"

Companionship in the Valley

It was a Sunday morning, a few years ago during a personal break that Donnie called. Answering immediately, I knew something was wrong. "Dad, dad, M is dead. This is so unfair dad." In a brief, painful conversation Donnie interrupted, "Dad, I have to go. The police need to talk with me." Within four hours we were at my son's house suffering alongside my family.

Maddening were well-meaning Christians trying to hit the high note of reason for the tragedy. Why do we feel the need to fix everything? The truth of "And we know that God causes everything to work together for the good . . ." was ill-timed and poorly delivered. Sounding their trumpets of reason and comfort, most failed to understand, words were not needed. They inflicted trauma, adding more pain not less. What we needed was presence. Sit with us. Feel with us.

112

Suffer with us. Hurt with us. Cry with us. Be quiet with us. But, please, please, please, right now shut up! Stop playing your trumpets people. Your high notes are off key and wounding our souls rather than helping. Please, enough! For right now anyways.

For my son and his wife who tried to revive the little one until the medics arrived, souls wreathed in pain. Thoughts and feelings wept, *"I cry out to God; yes, I shout. Oh, that God would listen to me! When I was in deep trouble, I searched for the Lord . . . but my soul was not comforted."* (Psalm 77:1-2) Faith was in crisis. For someone who's never experienced losing a child, no words can still this storm. Until you've pushed up and down on her little chest begging for life to return, please be careful with your words. Until you've entered our world, experienced our horror, please just suffer silently with us. Don't try to fix that which you do not understand.

Thankfully encouragement came. Firefighters who initially responded to the scene returned the next days. Their presence and words helped more than we expressed at the time. A police officer returned that evening and sat with family members. An Iraqi war vet medic just showed up and listened. And, we, our family rallied around each other. The hurting who hurt with us offered presence, not words filled with reason, Bible verses, and fixit theology. My gift connects me with others in a special way only suffering can accomplish. Initially scoring near a zero in mercy on a Spiritual Gifts test years ago, I rank high now. Suffering develops mercy and compassion.

Fight, Flight, or Flourish

Fight can embrace either victimization or support. How we view our struggles affects what we do with our anguish. My youngest brother, Robert, was diagnosed with Facial Scapular Muscular Dystrophy at the age of forty-two. Today he is limited to a wheel chair. He lived in a neighborhood frequented by the homeless. On a hot summer's day, you'd find him in that neighborhood in his wheel chair, handing out bottles of water to the homeless living in the streets of Northern, Minneapolis. His MD at the age of fifty-four, now forces him to an assisted living facility. Not a day goes by that my youngest brother doesn't suffer the pain from a disease eating his muscles away. In his pain, he writes poetry, shares encouragement, and tries to help struggling people around him. He's appeared on TV several times, and shared his poetry over the airwaves of local radio. He's one of the most positive people I know.

Flight runs from cause, solution, and possibilities. Preaching and teaching from time to time at Rescue Missions continually discovers scores of men just barely surviving in their unfortunate surroundings of life. Story after story paints a victim's picture of, "I'm only in this predicament because of what others did to me." Believing all their problems and suffering the result from ill treatment, many hide behind their well-rehearsed sad stories.

Flourish chooses to embark on an adventurous journey. The Huffington Post posted an article of sixteen hugely successful people, and the obstacles they overcame on their journey to success.[57] For example,

Bill Gates first business failed. Albert Einstein's teachers consider him a lazy dreamer always asking abstract questions people couldn't understand. Benjamin Franklin's parents couldn't afford to keep him in school past his tenth birthday. Richard Branson struggles with dyslexia. Stephen King's first novel, Carrie, was rejected dozens of times by publishers until finding acceptance. Thomas Edison failed almost 10,000 times before discovering the light bulb. Charlize Theron, witnessed her mother kill her father in self-defense. Stephen Spielberg was rejected by USC – University of Southern California; twice! Today he serves as one of its trustees. Simon Cowell suffered many failures in his rise to the top. Vincent Van Gogh sold only one painting in his lifetime.[58] His painting, L'Allée des Alyscamps recently sold at a Sotheby's auction for 66.3 million dollars.[59]

Ponderings

1. How do you personally make sense of your suffering?

2. How do you view suffering of others?

3. Through what lenses do you view your suffering?

4. How do you respond to suffering? Fight, Flight, or Freeze?

5. What's your thought about suffering possibly becoming a gift?

-10-
Soul-Forgiveness
Freedom of Releasing

"The weak can never forgive.
Forgiveness is the attribute of the strong."[60]
Mahatma Gandhi

"Always forgive your enemies - nothing annoys them so much."[61]
Oscar Wilde

"I can forgive, but I cannot forget, is only another way of saying,
I will not forgive."
Henry Ward Beecher

Simon Dube

Simon Dube taught me how to hit the high note of forgiveness. Whenever struggling to forgive someone for whatever perceived offense, I remember Simon Dube. His personal example of forgiving was the noblest self-sacrificing example ever personally witnessed.

Upon arriving in South Africa in June of 1986, learning the Zulu language was a high priority. There were no Zulu language schools to speak of, and learning the language depended on acquiring a tutor. A neighbor introduced me to Simon Dube.

The White Apartheid government forced rural Zulu communities off their traditional lands during the 60's and 70's. Simon grew up in his traditional family homestead in Roosboam. He played in view of the "big trees" where underneath four generations of family members were buried. That all changed when the government forcibly removed the entire population of several thousand, relocating them into small concrete block shanties in Ezakheni. The name "Ezakheni" meant, "We build together." Its name hid a dark history. Simon often mentioned the town name really meant, "We suffer together."

The small, thin, ageing Zulu man near 70 years old, agreed to teach me his language. Lessons began as a lifelong friendship ensued. Three months after our first lesson, Simon invited me to his home just outside Ladysmith. During our visit, Simon shared their story. Several times he interjected in his soft-spoken English, "We are all suffering here." Simon detailed the extent of his suffering, and that of his family, under the government. His single goal was, "To return to my family's place in Roosboom." With ten people crammed into a four room 600 sq. ft. house in that crowded shanty town, who could blame him.

Simon taught me the intricate Zulu language of clicks. It took years. As I learned to converse in his mother tongue, I began to see and understand his heart. As the missionary coming from America to teach the truths of Jesus, I think Simon taught me more about Christ. The missionary became the student never able bestow as much in return. Simon's immense capacity for forgiveness overwhelmed me at times. To Simon, the government was an oppressor. Simon "prayed for their leaders every day." He added, "I forgive them (then inflecting his voice upwards) for what they are doing to us." Listening to Simon pricked my heart in my own struggles to forgive a wayward father's many offenses. Simon added one of his many personalized Zulu proverbs,

"Unless one prays, one stays suffering in their heart."

As a theologically trained, ordained religious leader, Simon drilled into my own angry deep cavern. Once I enquired, "Baba, but how can one forgive when deeply hurt by another?" Learning about Zulu culture, I ceased calling Simon by his first name. This was a practice of many whites in South Africa. Simon's Zulu name, Mdlandlankulu, was unpronounceable to most whites, so he was just known as Simon. Calling an elder Zulu man by his first name among his people was highly disrespectful. "Baba," marked a term of respect given to all older Zulu men. Baba looked at me answering my question;

"Only in forgiving can a wounded soul find rest."

Simon, a WWII veteran, spent three years in an Italian POW camp, and in 1944 was moved to a German POW facility. His suffering was immense in those camps. He spoke very little about his captors or the experiences. He simply would say, "I prayed for the guards. What they were doing to us hurt them too. They held their soul's captive to by their own evilness." Once, a German guard let Baba pray with him. He simply said about the encounter, while other's souls were dying . . .

"Forgiving kept my soul alive."

Simon became more of a "Mfundisi" or pastor to me than I was to him. When Baba gave me a Zulu name, our relationship found a new depth. When just the two of us met together, he called me "Jabulani." Jabulani means "to rejoice." Apparently, our friendship brought happiness to Baba, as it did to me. Occasionally Baba looked announcing, "Jabulani, let's talk about forgiveness today. I think your soul needs it." Baba was right. Deep within the recesses of my heart a battle raged on towards my father's neglect, abuse, and abandonment. When speaking of "dad" Baba noted a changing angry demeanor protruding from my person. Baba would add another one of his personal Zulu proverbs,

"In anger a soul dies, only in forgiveness does a soul survive."

Baba knew a lot about survival. Every day of his life he awoke trying to survive one more day, and provide for his family. Baba read his new friend's heart well. Deep within anger lurked desiring release. The first five years, Baba and Jabulani spoke often about forgiveness. Jabulani prayed forgiveness towards his father many times, but it never seemed to connect with that white missionary's heart. Their relationship so free now, Jabulani admitted, "No matter how often I ask God to help me forgive my American father, anger is still present." Baba just smiled and said,

"Loving forgiveness more than your anger will set your soul free."

Baba's Zulu proverbs hit the mark. Living in anger somehow offered a level satisfaction I'd grown accustom to. I enjoyed my anger towards my father. It marked retribution for not being present during the football game I scored four touchdowns. I was always the kid whose parents never showed up; for anything. Baba scouted this anger, bringing my attention to it frequently. He'd admonish, *"Jabulani, until you love forgiving more than your fire, anger and bitterness, your soul will never be free."* One day marked a new depth of our friendship. Baba always chose to use the word "umlilo" or "fire" to describe anger and bitterness. To him, in his old Zulu language of metaphors, anger began as a small fire soon raging out of control.

Sitting in his cramped asbestos roof shack, he initiated another conversation on forgiveness. Before long he stood up and motioned, "Come, let's take a walk." Five houses down a dirt path outside his home, we stood in front of another shanty. Standing there, Baba began telling another one of his protracted stories. He began, "You see Jabulani, we both have a big problem. Fires burn in both our souls. Anger has too much power in us." As I began to counter, Baba raise his hand indicating silence desired by him on my part. He continued for quite some time explaining the house before us was that of the Vilakazi family. Standing animosities between the Dube and Vilakazi family were well known in Ezakheni section B.

Baba continued, "A few years before you arrived, my son was murdered before my eyes in front of my home." Baba told the story of his oldest son's argument with Vilakazi's oldest son. As he tried to separate the two young men, Vilakazi struck his son's head with a large rock. The blow to his head shattered his son's skull. Baba in graphic detail told of the 30-minute journey to the hospital in Ladysmith. With bit and pieces of his son's brain matter oozing onto his lap. Baba let out a deep breath and looked directly at me, "The power of my fire with Vilakazi is stronger than my forgiveness." In all our talk of Baba's heroic acts of forgiveness, he suffered an ultimate violent loss. Looking straight into my eyes, an unusual practice among older Zulu men, Baba said,

"The greatest battle to forgive is bound in one's deepest hurt."

As the oldest member of his Dube Clan, Baba duties pointed towards revenge. "Ukuphindisela" to repeat or "Ukubuyisela" to return back, marked a generation's old practice of retribution and revenge.

Once, a young Zulu pastor called me. In brokenness, he shared over the phone his father's murder. After the funeral, authorities discovered the father's murder was a revenge killing from a rival clan. The gory murder repaid a previous family killing that took place three generations earlier.

In Baba's case, his family expected their "Mkhulu," elder clansman, to lead in a plan for vengeance. Baba pondered in his broken English, "How does I do this?" Amid all our talk of forgiveness, my reasons for anger with my father appeared rather insignificant by comparison. Baba faced his greatest battle. To forgive his son's killer. In anguish, he recounted that horrendous day, Baba's words rang out:

"Until one loves forgiving more than the fire of anger,
a soul can never be released."

We agreed to spend considerable time together in prayer, asking God for help and guidance on the issue. Baba's handling of the Vilakazi – Dube feud feared implication of a small clan war.

Several weeks later, Baba approached me announcing, "Mfundisi, I did it." A puzzled look on my face asked for explanation. He continued, "I've dealt with the Vilakazi family." With reservation I replied, "You did what?" A pause, then in concern, "Baba, what did you do?" Baba told there and then the most incredible story of forgiveness and bravery.

Several days earlier, Baba approached the Vilakazi home. Walking up the short path to the door, someone in the home drew the curtains inside the small windows. Baba knocked on Vilakazi's door. "Sikhulekile ekhaya" – the old Zulu saying with many meanings always seemed to imply a sense of peace when approaching. As Baba knocked, repeating the saying, neighbors noted the event. Not a single person in Ezakheni section B was unaware of Vilakazi – Dube's coming war. As Baba knocked, a wrinkle of the curtain indicated someone inside observed the small skinny Zulu man just outside the door. After a few minutes, Baba began to sing. Zulu people express every emotion of life in song and melody. As Baba sang waiting outside the door, a small group of neighbors began to gather outside the gate of the Khumalo home.

He began singing, "Ngihlanze Emoyeni Wami," I Cleanse My Soul or Spirit. The small group growing in numbers outside the gate, joined in three-part harmony. Zulus sing to mark just about every occasion of life. In birth, life, and death, Zulus sing. In political struggle, they sing. Their harmony is unique, led often by a lead singer, and driven by deep male bass vocals. That day was marked by melody rather than conflict.

Before long better than 50 neighbors stood outside the gate in that crowed shanty town singing with Baba. Just then, the metal door cracked open, and behind the opening stood old man Vilakazi. Ten years elder to Baba, he asked politely, "Ufunani lapha?" What do you want here? After the normal custom of greeting each other, strictly held to by rural Zulu people, Baba announced his intentions.

Two old men peering through a door's crack, Baba began, "You know the offense the Vilakazi family committed against we Dube's." As one neighbor described the entire scene weeks later, most believed a declaration of hostilities to follow. Baba's words startled everyone that day unexpectedly. He continued, "Your grandson took something from us Dube's that can never be returned. We live with the pain of our son's loss every day. Nothing we say or do will bring my son back to me. But I choose to "Thela Amanzi" this day with our families. The phrase "Thela Amanzi" literally means to "pour out the water." The saying pointed to earlier times in Zulu culture when a peace treaty or agreement was reached. The leader of each tribe or clan poured out water unto the ground in a ceremonial declaration of peace.

Upon, "Thela Amanzi" old man Vilakazi opened his door widely. Baba greeted him again, announcing, "Thina sonke saphile," or "we are all well today." The conversation now began in earnest. Baba continued in front of a large group outside the gate "Our pain continues, but the Dube fire is gone. I announced this day, that I, Simon Dube, instruct my family to offer the hand of peace to all Vilakazi's. Revenge ends today." From eyewitness accounts, Baba's words stunned the ever-increasing crowd. He continued,

"I offer forgiveness that I hope my enemies might extend to me."

Reaching out his hand, he continued, "If my son killed your son, I'd stand where you stand today. We offer your family forgiveness." Old man Vilakazi took Baba's hand. A chorus of rejoicing broke out among the crowd. And, here's the truly miraculous part of the story. That following Sunday, the entire Vilakazi family sat in church up front with Baba Dube's family. This included the young man who killed Baba's son. It was, and still is, one of the most amazing things I've ever witnessed. Simon often commented after the episode;

"Forgiving released my soul to live free."

Talking later after that incredible week, several realities emerged. Talking about forgiveness in the church, doesn't appear to connect often with church people. We talked a good forgiveness-game, but most of us are lousy forgivers. Behind many soul's boiler plates rages angry fires of self-reasoned justified unforgiveness. **Whenever I struggle to forgive, I think of Simon Dube's Forgiveness.**

This pastor witnessed over the years "Christians" slay each other for far less. A conclusion reached long ago through observation is that many people in the church carry much anger. Fires burn deep within their souls. Flames of animosity directed towards others often seethe behind many smiles. The highest percentage of sessions with married couples almost always involve that "fire" Baba described. A self-satisfying and self-gratifying rage burns deep below. People hang onto their "fire" towards others. It's almost a way of personal retribution. The fire taints every other experience searing the very fabric of the soul.

Unforgiveness carries severe consequences. Jesus noted, *"If you forgive those who sin against you, your heavenly Father will forgive you. But if you refuse to forgive others, your Father will not forgive your sins."* (Matthew 6:14-15)

The Forgiveness Continuum

The Cambridge Dictionary defines "continuum" as, "something that changes in character gradually or in very slight stages without any clear dividing points."[62] Rarely, does once experience complete release at a first offer of forgiveness. That's my experience anyways.

Forgiveness doesn't appear to possess clear dividing points at times. In my own personal journey, forgiveness seems a process of spiritual growth. The greater the offense, the longer the process of granting complete forgiveness.

Why Should I?

Do it for yourself. When encouraging a person to forgive another often is asked, "Why should I forgive?" Have you ever watched someone talk about another person, and the longer they talked, the angrier they became? Unforgiveness affects you more than him / her / or them.

Paul wrote a letter to a church in Ephesus Greece about this very thing. Apparently, within that congregation sat some very angry people. He commanded them, *"Get rid of all bitterness, rage, anger, harsh words, and slander, as well as all types of evil behavior."* (Ephesians 4:31) Notice the progression:

bitterness → rage → anger → harsh words → slander → evil behavior

Do it for others. In modern usage, "slander" is generally understood as making untrue and damaging statements about another person. The word Paul used here means much more. "Slander" in Ephesians 4:31, comes from the Greek word "blasphemia." Perhaps you recognize it? English transliterates the word to "blasphemy." Towards the end of a self-destructive downward spiral of unforgiveness, slander blasphemes others. Have you ever considered when speaking negatively about another person, you blaspheme that person? Total forgiveness circumvents blasphemy.

Do it for God. Slander, blashphemia, is directed towards God. When I choose to slander another person, my actions affect more than just a few words of spoken malice. Slander wounds my soul, injures both myself and another, and puts myself at odds with my Creator.

A better alternative. There's something satisfying in carrying malice towards an offender. It feels like a way to get back. Problem is, malice and anger usually devour the offended; not the offender. Anger empowers an offender to live within my soul. I allow my offender this power. Paul offers a better alternative, "Instead, be **kind** to each other, **tenderhearted, forgiving** one another, just as God through Christ has forgiven you." (Ephesians 4:31-32) The question regularly lashes back, "But, why must I be the one to forgive?" Because unforgiveness leads to anger. When it reaches slander, we become the offenders.

Our soul wars against the whole notion of forgiving a guilty wronging person. Doesn't it? But, if I choose to forgive someone who's wronged me, it **releases them from the inner recesses of my heart. When I let the hurt go, I can let them go too.**

There's something self-satisfying in hanging onto an offense. Playing it repeatedly in one's soul. As we replay an offense, it develops into a fiction story not resembling the true facts. The offense grows into a full-blown motion picture within our souls failing to reflect the accuracy of the actual event.

When my oldest son was fourteen, living in South Africa, he and his best friend, Chris, loved the movie Dumb and Dumber. Watching the movie numerous times, they acted out various scenes in hilarious accuracy. Then they began to rewrite the script in their dialogues. In greater comicality, Dumb and Dumber became Dumb, Dumber, Dumbest, and Dumber still.

When listening to someone tell of an offense committed against them, inaccuracies always occur. Constantly I asked, "What did that person actually say?" Or, "Take me through the events from the beginning of what that person actually did." Upon deconstruction of their story, many inaccuracies surfaced.

Let's admit it, it feels good to hang on to our pain and injury. Doesn't it? That way we get back. We can extract reckoning from the offender. At least in our minds. Some of the angriest, most miserable people I've ever known suffer from bitter, twisted souls recounting offenses decades old. There's a high personal price to pay for this.

Replaying an offense repeatedly allows an offender to bully us on our own playground. Every day is ruined because the bully is always there. We fear going to our playground. The imaginary bully creates fear and anger. That bully is really you. When harboring offenses, you are your own bully.

Forgiveness sends your bully packing. Forgiveness clears your soul. Forgiveness brings releasing. Releasing brings freedom. It's up to you.

Forgiveness Reflects God's Actions Towards Me

In forgiving, I develop my soul to resemble my creator. This is helpful when dealing with continual feelings of betrayal, harm, or injury at the hands of another person. Once a woman asked for guidance, "I forgive him today, but when I wake up tomorrow, I know I'll be angry with him again." Practice forgiveness! Offer a prayer of forgiveness every time a thought of bitterness, pain, or anger wells up towards another person. Forgiveness rarely marks a single solitary event. It should, but rarely does this happen in our fallen natures. It's a continual process seeping into the nooks and crannies of the soul.

Forgiveness Takes Practice

The eruptive Peter comes to Jesus asking, "Lord, how often should I forgive someone who sins against me? Seven times?" Let's rephrase the question in modern language, "So, Jesus, hey, if I forgive someone who's knocked me down seven times, that's pretty generous. Right? What do you think?" I sort of imagine Peter standing, feeling rather smug with his statement. In fact, to think about it a bit, Peter's offer of forgive someone seven times is generous. Ask yourself, **"When is the last time I forgave an individual seven times for seven offenses?"**

That spouse who cheated on you – 7 times? The father who abandoned you – 7 times? The lies and untruths told about you – 7 times? The injury caused to you – 7 times? Peter's question to forgive 7 times surpasses most of our willingness to forgive. Personally, I find Peter's forgiveness question challenging.

Jesus blew Peter out of the water with his response, *"I do not say to you seven times, but seventy-seven times."* (Matthew 18:21-22). I bet conniptions and convulsions took place in the bombastic Peter's heart over this one! It's not the first time Jesus states the practically impossible. In another instance, Jesus qualifies forgiveness.

Forgiveness Requested is Forgiveness Granted

Jesus raised the bar to a seemingly impossible height. *"If another believer sins, rebuke that person; then if there is repentance, forgive. Even if that person wrongs you seven times a day and each time turns again and asks forgiveness, you must forgive him."* (Luke 17:4) You must forgive. 7 x 70? Really, Jesus? The number "7" represents completion or fulfillment. Rabbis often taught in Jesus day, to forgive a person three times fulfilled God's requirement. Amos 1:3-13, seems to indicate some reasoning for this position.

Forgiveness Rarely Practiced

I received a call that a certain man in our congregation died. Unknown, he made up one of the many "Who use to go to your church." His wife, a most disagreeable woman on the best of days, made demands in the planning of the funeral. She insisted a certain relative be barred from entering the church if he attempted to attend the funeral. Upon my

131

refusal to act as a bouncer rather than a pastor conducting a funeral, she angrily protested. She found a "more suitable" church for the funeral. Sure enough, that outlawed relative tried to attend the funeral. He was aggressively rebuffed at the door, and turned away. All this, while the deceased's favorite hymn played in the sanctuary, "Amazing Grace." You can't make this stuff up.

My frustration with the woman turned to empathy and pity. Living in such rancor, every member of that family lived handcuffed to a smoldering pit of familial ruin. Simon Dube's Forgiveness came to mind. In the very church with so many prayers offered, forgiveness was nowhere in sight.

Have you ever thought, "What are the results of my refusal to forgive?" The Twelve, Jesus' chosen, often argued. Disagreements over position, status, and stature were topics of disagreement. Even during the Last Supper, marking the eve of his incarceration and death, an argument broke out between them. As Jesus shared his pain, the Twelve focused on personal gain. "Then they began to argue among themselves about who would be the greatest among them." (Matthew 22:24) Not much has changed two thousand years later. Church leaders continue to fight and divide over status, name, position, and politics.

Forgiveness is Key to Answered Prayer

Jesus makes a promise, *"I tell you, you can pray for anything, and if you believe that you've received it, it will be yours."* There is a caveat to his promise however. *"But when you are praying, **first forgive** anyone you are holding a grudge against, so that your Father in heaven **will forgive***

132

your sins, too." (Mark 11:24-25) Note verse twenty-four is conditional upon verse-twenty-five.

Prayer Absent Forgiveness – Just Words

The Bible reminds us to pray often. Jesus centered his disciples upon their need for continuous prayer, *"One day Jesus told his disciples a story to show that they should **always pray** and never give up."* (Luke 18:1) In always praying forgiveness is top priority.

In the Lord's Prayer, Jesus teaches his disciples, *"This is how you should pray . . ."* "Pray," implies a regular activity. Jesus reminded, *"And forgive us our sins, as we have forgiven those who sin against us."* Forgiveness is to be a regular active function of prayer. In the Lord's Prayer, forgiveness is foundational to connecting with God. Perhaps the reason that many sitting in the church struggle with anger, bitterness, and resentment is directly attributable to a weak ineffective prayer life. Is unforgiveness the cause of many weak, ineffective prayers that go unanswered?

On a Wednesday night, I sat with a family during pizza night at church. Within a few minutes of sitting down, mom with two children began to tell a story. For more than an hour she recounted episode after episode of injustices committed by her mother and two sisters. The more she talked, the angrier she grew. Other's noticed her increasing explosive demeanor. Her pastor gently posed three questions.

Do your sisters feel you've offended them too? She responded, "Well, I suppose so." Do you desire your sisters to drop their reasons for their offense with you? She again responded, "Well, yah, I suppose so."

Can you offer your mother and sisters the same forgiveness you hope they might extend you? Standing up and heading for Wednesday night activities she answered, "I'll have to think about that one."

I offered a thought. Can you look at that person more than their offense? She never returned to the church she belonged to for over ten years. Her resentment and bitterness revealed a prayerless forgiveless soul bound. The fire within ravaged her soul far more than the offenders' offenses.

My Personal Forgiveness Continuum

In the Lord's Prayer, Jesus words speak out to me, "*. . . so that your Father in heaven will forgive your sins, too.*" During the writing of Son Risings, a letter arrived in my box at the Post Office. Reading the return address on the envelope, I saw it was from the church I resigned my senior pastorate just eighteen months prior to begin Missionary to Missionary Care. To say I left that church wounded and debilitated is an understatement. Before my acceptance as Senior Pastor, the pastor before me stayed only 18 months. Prior to that pastor marked a tenure by another pastor of only 9 months. After my departure, a new pastor survived just 3 months. I managed to last 5 years! Some of my final words to the elder board of that church were, "Perhaps, the problem with your church is not your pastors, but you yourselves?" Trying to finish well, my last message on a Sunday morning was one of forgiveness. Cold stone faces stared motionless as I offered forgiveness towards "offenders" present that morning. A genuine offer of forgiveness received with a shrug of the collective church body's shoulders added to the weight of feeling used up and discarded. At any rate, I'd done my part. Or, so I thought.

Our five years there proved quite an irony. On the one hand, most the church folk loved and cared for us. A good many of them provided the labor to construct our home. High hopes for a long-term tenure flourished. And, we enjoyed our new house in the woods just 40 minutes from the lake where my grandfather taught me to fish. Things looked good, but . . .

As I dragged out of that town, I didn't know if any room in my heart existed to ever trust people again. I remember thinking driving the U-Haul Truck towards my oldest son's home in Wisconsin, "You know God, I really hate some of those people." Hate towards a few overpowered the goodness of the many in that church.

A pastor friend in South Africa from the Dutch Reformed Church, totally wrung out said in my younger years, "Don, you know, I really hate Christians sometimes." Beat up, worn out, and depleted clergy rarely speak of the ravages they suffer at the hands of their memberships. It's one of the great secrets of the church. It's the reason many churches can't keep a pastor long term. And, it's the reason many smaller churches sit pastorless today throughout America's church landscape. What some "Christians" do to their pastors is a traumatic tragedy.

In all my life, over twenty years in Africa, ten years pastoring in the United States, and growing up in an alcoholics' home, it's was the first time I ever remembered hating someone. I knew it was wrong. I knew God was unpleased. But, that's how I felt. I called some of those people the Gang of Thirty. Thirty or so individuals in that congregation successfully and covertly ran off six other pastors over a twenty-year span. Thirty people over shadowed five-hundred good people. With only one exception, every pastor sought secular employment, leaving pastoral ministry for good; after that church.

As I opened the envelope, my hands began to sweat, my stomach bunched up inside, and my heart raced. Just thinking about the Gang of Thirty produced a hundred emotions. Mostly of fear, resentment, and anger. Removing the letter and opening it, I read the one-page letter offering an apology by the elder board for not "protecting" me during my tenure as pastor. The elder board acknowledged their shortcomings and sins against me.

My first thoughts were angry. "Really! After everything that happened you're just going to send a letter?" Secondary thoughts accused, "What a cowardly way to ask forgiveness!" Then my heart turned towards judging, "Your interim pastor probably led you to do this. Without his encouragement, or insistence, you'd never come around to this by yourselves." I began setting conditions of accepting and granting forgiveness, "You stand before YOUR church in front of YOUR people and YOUR families, and admit this, THEN we might have something to talk about!" Besides, I made my gesture of forgiveness during my sermon on my last Sunday. I've done my part. Really?

1st The Forgiving Simon Dube

You know what? Simon Dube's offer of forgiveness those many years ago to the murderer of his son often spoke to my soul immediately.

Yes, those members of the Gang of Thirty hurt me. They were wrong. No doubt about it. They sinned against me. But, now my problem was no longer them. My problem was me. The anger I harbored against them came to the surface in my full view with that letter. Contemplating the contents of the letter, and noting the many signatures brought both smiles and consternation. My heart simply wasn't willing to forgive. **Feelings ruled forgiveness.** Standing in the Post Office reading that confessional letter of forgiveness, I remembered Simon Dube:

> *"Until one loves forgiving more than the fire of anger,*
> *a soul can never be released."*

Simon's willingness to forgive an ultimate offense of man who killed his son, was an inescapable example of forgiveness. It was as if Simon spoke out to me, "Don (Jabulani) you can do this. You must do this."

2nd God's Incredible Gift

The most famous verse in the Bible begins, *"For God loved the world so much that he **gave** his only Son . . ."* (John 3:16a). Woven into the fabric of the Bible, proclamations of God's love repeat themselves. This love is described as, *"God is so rich in mercy, and he loved us so much . . .* (Ephesians 2:4a). Repeatedly, God reminds of his immense compassion and plan for us, *"So God can point to us in all future ages as examples of the incredible wealth of his grace and kindness toward us, as shown in all he has done for us who are **united with Christ Jesus**."* (Ephesians 2:7). Since God's layers his compassion through His Son, it encourages personal reciprocation. In the very least, I can forgive because I am forgiven. *"Remember, the Lord forgave you, so you must forgive others."* (Colossians 3:13).

3rd Unforgiveness – Not an Option

Jesus words pierced me, *"Forgive us **our sins** are we forgive those who trespassed against us."* Learned in catechism as a young boy, the words pursued, "Don, what about your sins here?" The battle raged, "But God, do you know how many pastors they've hurt? Do you know the deceit and wickedness in some of those 'leaders' in that church? Do you know the lies they told about me, the cover-ups, and all the rest? I did my bit in my last message. I offered forgiveness and requested forgiveness on that last Sunday. Why, God, continue to pester me with it now?" Then, in almost an audible voice God spoke, "Because Don, you're still sinful, angry, hateful, and bitter towards those people." Exhaling deeply, I whispered standing in the Post Office, "Ok, I guess God, here we go again. I, I, I, well, I . . . forgive them. A g a i n . . .

One thing I've learned over almost forty years of ministry is that pastors, church leaders, and missionaries confess little, and forgive less. I am an efficient grudge holder at times. While maintaining innocence, I still needed to come face to face with my bitterness. John's words pounded, *"If someone says, "I love God," but hates a Christian brother or sister, that person is a liar; for if we don't love people we can see, how can we love God, whom we cannot see?"* (1 John 4:20) During my entire five-year exchange with those people, my sin of hatred stood as the most depraved of any sin committed in that congregation. The pastor, stood most guilty of all. "Hatred" here in this verse is in the present tense and active voice. This indicates an active living emotion working within one's soul. My hatred towards the Gang of Thirty was certainly present and active.

Here's the thing. For Christians, unforgiveness is not an option. For pastors wronged by their membership, unforgiveness finds no justification. For missionaries, unappreciated and forgotten, unforgiveness is the wrong cave to crawl into and dwell. True humility forgives. Leaders who experienced betrayal, unforgiveness is the worst of companions.

Now, perhaps forgiveness follows a long path through one's soul before finally reaching its destination. Ultimately, for a follower of Christ, forgiveness is expected. God demands it. And, we need its releasing freedom. I'm convinced this is one of the reasons Jesus commanded us to forgive. His words pounded me in Luke 17:4, **"Even if that person wrongs you seven times a day and each time turns again and asks forgiveness, you _must forgive_ him."** (Luke 17:4) When Jesus said, *"You must forgive,"* he spoke in the future tense. What Christ was saying is, "You will forgive because he will offend." Forgiveness then becomes a decision of the will rather than an emotion to be acted upon.

Don, are you going to forgive? Well, I don't feel like forgiving those people – that person. So what? Are you forgiven? Have you experienced God's grace in Jesus Christ for the forgiveness of sins? Do you wish to be forgiven by others when you commit an offense? Forgiveness – there is no other option. Someone spoke to my soul that day in the Post Office, "Don you are going to forgive. Do it. Or, . . ."

I struggled, "But . . . Jesus, I just can't . . . I just want to forget about the whole thing." Not forget about those member's offenses against me, but rather forget about my pressing need to forgive. "God, I just want to forget forgiving." With that I tore the letter up, threw it into the waste basket at the Post Office and left.

Simon Dube's example and Christ's words nudged my soul often, "Time to let it go Don. Release it." Knowing forgiveness was granted to me, and that mere gratitude demanded reciprocation, still I struggled. Considering the Scriptures, I found what I like to call "The Instead Factor."

The Instead Factor

Pondering that letter over a period of several weeks, no, several months, God and Simon Dube's examples of forgiveness blew across my soul's bow repeatedly. A friend reminded me of a verse in the Bible I'd taught on many times, *"**Instead**, be kind to each other, tenderhearted, forgiving one another, just as God through Christ has forgiven you."* (Ephesians 4:32) My friend looked me straight in the eye and said, "Don, it's time. Instead of searing your soul upon a hot rock of anger and bitterness, replace it with the spiritual formula here in this verse.

'The Crucifixion' by Rubens, Pieter Paul (1577-1640), portrays Christ attached to the cross by three nails. Affixing Christ's limbs to the cross resembles rugged spikes more than the smooth shinny penny nails available today. The visual aid of three pitted jagged spikes driven through Christ's hands and feet offers a stunning visual reason to forgive. As I visualized Christ dangling from those nails withering in pain offering the words, *"Father, forgive them, they know not what they do,"* I can

140

forgive. Replacing my hurt, pain, and anger with my Savior hanging on that old rugged cross leaves no reason to live forgiveless.

Three Nails Instead Factor.

First Nail – Be kind. Instead of bitterness, rage, anger, harsh words, and slander, INSTEAD all that negative stuff. Replace it with kindness towards people. All people. Offending people. Grumpy people. Hurtful people. When thoughts of anger towards The Gang of Thirty surfaced, offering kindness towards someone helped my soul. Kindness forced unforgiveness from my soul. It offered freedom from imprisoned feelings and thoughts of malice and vengeance towards another person.

"Kind," in Ephesians 4:32, carries the idea of being easy going, not harsh, hard, sharp or caustic towards people.[63] "Bible Believing Christians" often mark themselves by harshness towards others. In fact, the harshest people I've ever known tend to be "Bible Believing Christians." Schooled in the Scriptures, they tend to swing their Bible knowledge like a sledge with zero grace. The application here of "Be Kind" represents people who are useful, suitable, affectionate, and friendly.[64] When struggling with forgiveness, the first nail reminds that kindness displaces anger.

Second Nail – Be tenderhearted. "Tenderhearted" is a strange word coming the Greek word, "splagchnon" and literally means "having strong, healthy bowels." It is a rare word, and used only two times in Scripture. To the Greeks and Romans, one's bowls represented the deepest most inward part of a human being. A modern equivalent might be, "I feel it in the pit of my stomach."[65] Many songs in American music reflect "splagchnon" describing feelings of love deep within one's heart.

To be "splagchnon" towards someone entails a broken-hearted and deep-seated feeling of affection towards people. "Tenderhearted" means to be easily moved towards love, pity, or sorrow for someone else.[66] Instead of anger and slander towards an offender, I must choose to replace caustic evil feelings with "splagchnon." Tenderheartedness softens and purifies a soul towards people.

3rd Nail – Forgiving. To forgive, literally means to give freely and unconditionally as a gift. Or, to wipe clean a debt someone owes you. Notice, the word "**forgiving**" is in the present tense meaning offering forgiveness is a continual on-going act. The picture here is one of taking off an old dirty shirt replacing it with a clean garment. Just a few verses prior Paul encourages, *"put off your old self – put on the new self."* (Ephesians 4:22 & 24 NIV)

The Three Nails of Instead, encourages us to throw of the old self of living in hurt, injury, and pain. **Kindness, Tenderheartedness,** and **Forgiveness** sets a soul free. The fire that Simon spoke of so many years ago dwindles with forgiveness. And, if that's not enough, the last words of Ephesians 4:32 brings the whole matter to a nonnegotiable conclusion. *"Just as God through Christ has forgiven you."*

Here's the thing. Only God can completely forgive sin. My responsibility is to forgive the offender. God deals with the actual sin. The Bible is clear on this, *"God will judge us for everything we do, including every secret thing, whether good or bad."* (Ecclesiastes 12:4) Constantly,

142

it does good to remind oneself that it's God's job to forgive sin, *"But if we confess our sins to him, he is faithful and just to forgive us our sins and to cleanse us from all wickedness."* Only God possesses the power to forgive people of their sins. Our responsibility is to release both the offender and the offended through forgiveness. *"Make allowance for each other's faults, and forgive anyone who offends you. Remember, the Lord forgave you, so you must forgive others."* (Colossians 3:13)

God spoke to me, "Now, Don, write down every name of the person of the Gang of Thirty. Everyone." The next morning, the Gang of Thirty existed in ink within the pages of my journal. God continued, "Now, every person, every name, pray for each one of them offering forgiveness, and asking for My best in their lives."

Certain names proved easier to offer forgiveness than others. Over a period of a year, finally, with the last name, a most unpleasant woman I despised, every person was released from my cave; almost. God spoke again, "That woman, your arch nemesis, the one who hurt you the deepest, I want you to pray for her every day for the next year." So, as I write these words, that woman surfaces in my soul every day. My soul-response is one of forgiveness, blessings, and release. She is freed from my soul to torment me no longer!

That's the end of the matter of that letter in the Post Office. I think. It was as if God said, "Don, you are going to forgive. Forgive those people. Let me deal with them. Release your injury, pain, and desires for retribution. Experience the freedom forgiveness offers." Releasing those offenders and their offenses from my soul's radar, brought the freedom my soul sought. Martin Luther King Jr.'s words rang out, "Free at last, free at last, thank God Almighty, we are free at last."

Ponderings

1. How does Simon Dube's story of forgiveness impact you?

2. What resonates with you from Simon's words:

    "Forgiving releases a soul to live free."

3. How might you experience release in forgiveness? Release from what?

4. The Forgiveness Continuum presents forgiveness as a process of spiritual growth. Describe your personal growth in your own Forgiveness Continuum.

5. Forgive 7 x 70 – Thoughts?

6. Again, what speaks to your soul in Simon Dube's Words:

   "The greatest battle to forgive is bound in one's deepest hurt."

7. Does the Instead Factor of Ephesians 4:31-32 resonate with you? If so, how? If not, why?

8. What truth does the Three Nails of kindness, tenderheartedness, and forgiving present?

-11-
Soul-Renewal
Learning to Quiet Your Soul

"Be at peace with your own soul, then heaven and earth will be at peace with you."[67]
Isaac of Nineveh

"He restoreth my soul . . ."
Psalm 23:1 (KJV)

The Twenty-third Psalm is a well quoted passage of Scripture at funerals. This passage of Scripture has brought comfort to millions of grieving souls grappling with losing a loved one. I suppose there is no other passage better known, or more comforting than the Twenty-third Psalm. It's quite often quoted in the King James Version:

Soul Health

The Lord is my shepherd; I shall not want.
He maketh me to lie down in green pastures: he leadeth me beside the still waters.
*He **restoreth my soul**: he leadeth me in the paths of righteousness for his name's sake.*

Soul Living

Yea, though I walk through the valley of the shadow of death, I will fear no evil: for thou art with me; thy rod and thy staff they comfort me.
Thou preparest a table before me in the presence of mine enemies: thou anointest my head with oil; my cup runneth over.

Surely goodness and mercy shall follow me all the days of my life: and I will dwell in the house of the Lord forever.

Interestingly, the Twenty-third Psalm has very little to do with funerals. The ancient song speaks of the ingredients of a healthy soul. I like to divide them into two main sections; Soul Health and Soul Living. *"Shuwb"* is the Hebrew word translated in various translations, "Restore, renew, revive, or refresh." The Aramaic Bible in Plain English, translates the word, *"brings back my soul."* The emphasis in the first three verses of the 23rd Psalm is bringing back one's soul to health. Restoration, health, revitalization, and preparation is the focus of this wonderful psalm.

King David of Israel authored this Psalm. His life was marked by many highs and lows. From a young, maybe just 15 years old, simple shepherd boy caring for his father's sheep, David was catapulted into hero status. His slaying of Goliath in the Valley of Elah turned him instantly into both celebrity and enemy. King Saul, initially grateful, turns towards resentment, jealousy, and hatred. He views David as a threat to his throne. In the limelight of praise and adulation, Saul betrayed David. David lived as an outlaw, betrayed by his king, hunted as a criminal, and living throughout the caves of Israel. Fifteen long years pass before David took the throne after being anointed King. Initially, his rule was not harmonious. The war between Saul's house and David's throne lasted many years before David unified his rule. Imagine the impact of such strife, warring, and fighting upon David's soul. Hardly good preparation for a future king.

Here in the Twenty-third Psalm, David perhaps sat as Israel's king looking back on his life. Dealing with the stresses of kingship marked huge shifts from his shepherd days. By far the wealthiest and most powerful man in the nation, he grappled with the struggles of ruling a small kingdom surrounded by enemies aimed at wiping out the new little nation. The pressures were immense.

Perhaps he asked himself, "What is the one thing that kept me going while hiding in those caves? How did I survive all those valley battles? Through all the betrayals, marital problems, strife, and personal failures, what is the one thing that brought me to where I am today?" David looked back at his days shepherding in the fields of Judah.

Soul Health

In the first three verses, David experienced a time of soul refreshing. "Restore" here literally means to "bring back the soul." David sought to bring his soul to a healthier place amid incredible crushing pressures. David cried out, *"Have mercy on me, Lord, for I am in distress. Tears blur my eyes. My body and soul are withering away."* (Psalms 31:9). David's words cry out from the hearts of many today. David looked to his Shephard. To David, the soul – the real you, was not just a rarely ever considered just keep plugging along lifestyle. It was of the highest consideration. To cope with the stresses of life, the great king fixed his soul in four principles of health:

1st Connection with the Shepherd

"**The Lord is my shepherd . . .**" "Lord" here comes from the Hebrew word, "râ'âh" indicating many encouraging qualities of our shepherd. According to *Gesenius' Hebrew-Chaldee Lexicon*, "shepherd" means, "to feed, shepherd, or tend to a flock. As far as the origin of the word, it probably carries a sense of **looking upon . . . with pleasure.**" David wrote, *"My shepherd looks upon me with pleasure."*[68] David's connection with The Great Shepherd, brought him to a rich relationship of enjoyment. *"The Lord is my shepherd; he takes great pleasure in me."* Think about this for a moment. When was the last time you thought, "God takes pleasure in me?" Yes, David failed many times. In fact, he really dropped the ball a couple of times. So severe were his short comings that God stepped in radically to bring David, his sheep, back into the fold. Yet, God's pleasure in David's kept his soul connected to God. **Soul health requires a connection to someone or something greater than one's self.**

Our soul is shepherd-dependent. Without a shepherd, one's soul wanders into dangerous valleys unaware and exposed. Notice what David didn't say. He didn't say, "the lord is a shepherd." Many people ascribe some value or worth to God in their lives. David sited God as more than just an addition. David's shepherd statement is practical, personal, and absolute. The Shepherd was everything or nothing. Either a Shepherd leads, and a soul follows, or it wanders away. Forty years of missionary and pastoral work attests to many wandering souls calling out to a shepherd they are unwilling to follow. When faced with job loss, they reach out. When suffering a horrible divorce, look to the shepherd. Struggling with an addiction, call out to God. When that phone call comes from the doctor about an illness, "Help me God." In maladies of life, many turn to the shepherd. But, eventually, they wander off again to unsafe pastures into the clutches of the lion.

Many years living among Zulu rural villagers in South Africa taught there is nothing more helpless than sheep apart from the watchful eye of a shepherd. Whether in the high cool mountain air of Lesotho, or the hot valleys of Natal, sheep can't survive apart from their shepherd. Without their shepherd, sheep wander aimlessly into harm's way without a clue to their impending doom.

Once a young Zulu boy was disciplined by his father for not properly tending to his sheep. Distracted by other young Zulu boys, their sheep wandered off into the mountains. That Zulu boy, now an old man, told of a day when his family's sheep under his care were devoured by a small pack of black-backed jackals. He said, "Sheep by themselves never survive. If the shepherd tends to his sheep, they fear nothing, they know little of the danger all around them. A good shepherd leads his sheep through every event of their lives."

For David, as a young shepherd boy, well fed, healthy, and protected sheep offered a vivid picture of soul-care. Running from cave to cave chased by his king and enemies, constant strife marked David's life. In Psalms, depending upon the translation, "enemy" or "enemies" is mentioned over 100 times. Most people never think of the Psalms in relation to enemies. These enemies caused David worry, sadness, and frustration much of his life. Much of David's struggles in life directly correlated to his enemies. David sought his shepherd's care and guidance. Rather than wander aimlessly about driven by the winds of events, David chose to focus upon his guide for life. He stated this as a matter of fact.

We too experience enemies. Depression, anxiety, busyness, addiction, capacity, margin, strife, conflict, hatred, and a host of other adversaries seek to slay us in the dark caves of human challenges. In my challenges and down times of life, immense confidence gains footing in my soul by the thoughts, "The Lord is my shepherd – taking pleasure in me . . ."

2nd Contentment in the Shepherd

David adds to his absolute statement of personal fact, *"The LORD is my shepherd, I shall not want."* Literally, *"I do not lack."* (YLT) Quite an incredible statement for a king looking back to his young teenage shepherding years. Surrounded by power, authority, wealth, and pleasure, David boiled his life down to one essence. *"The Lord is my shepherd, in him, I have all I need."* The Shepherd's care for his sheep is a dominant theme. Sheep from different cultures thousands of years ago worried about this same stuff we do today; provision. Am I going to have enough? Look at just a few Bible verses reassuring a caring Shepherd cares for his sheep:

> Do not be afraid or discouraged, for the Lord will personally go ahead of you. He will be with you; he will neither fail you nor abandon you." (Deuteronomy 31:8)

Don't love money; be satisfied with what you have. For God has said, "I will never fail you. I will never abandon you." (Hebrews 13:5)

Commit everything you do to the LORD. Trust him, and he will help you. (Psalms 37:5)

And why worry about your clothing? Look at the lilies of the field and how they grow. They don't work or make their clothing, yet Solomon in all his glory was not dressed as beautifully as they are. And if God cares so wonderfully for wildflowers that are here today and thrown into the fire tomorrow, he will certainly care for you. (Matthew 6:28-30)

Don't worry about anything; instead, pray about everything. Tell God what you need, and thank him for all he has done. Then you will experience God's peace, which exceeds anything we can understand. His peace will guard your hearts and minds as you live in Christ Jesus. (Philippians 4:6-7)

Give all your worries and cares to God, for he cares about you. (1 Peter 5:7)

David's contentment in life linked directly to his shepherd. Picture, it. A king living in a lavish palace. Supplied with every desire at his beckoning. A leader among leaders revered around the world. David sourced life's meaning in the "Existing One" – the LORD his Shepherd. But, how did this King of Israel come to such a personal confident relationship with this Shepherd? The shepherd earned David's trust through constant care for his sheep.

3rd Care of the Shepherd

Get Some Rest. The Hebrew word for "Lie down" is *"rabats"* and is in the Hiphil stem. Some versions translate the phrase, *"He lets me rest*

. . ." (NTL) However, the verb stem points towards a causative more forceful, *"He makes me lie down . . ."* (NASB) The shepherd forces his sheep to take necessary rest. Rest is the dire need of our day in the American culture.

"Forty-five percent of Americans say that poor or insufficient sleep affected their daily activities at least once in the past seven days," according to the National Sleep Foundation.[69] In Brigid Schulte's book, *Overwhelmed, Work, Love and Play When No One Has the Time,* the writer for the Washington Post notes Americans obsession with busyness. She writes, "In the U.S., however, we have made a cult of busyness. Most of us limp by with just two weeks of vacation a year, and many of us don't even use that pitiful amount of time. We assign status based on who works the longest hours and gets the least sleep, even though other countries with 30-day vacations and limits on how long people can work have higher productivity rates."[70] Cara Heissman, Publisher of the Tiny Buddha, draws a correlation between extreme busyness and stress. "Being crazy-busy implies stress; and our body can only take so much pressure before it activates its stress response and runs on 'survival or panic mode.'"[71] Some of the most out of control people I know constantly flitter about hyperventilating from one place to another under the veil of busyness.

The shepherd realized that his sheep needed rest. He forced his sheep to do what they naturally did not do for themselves; rest. Blessed with 14 grandchildren, it's interesting to watch the battle for rest, which occurs when mom or dad announces bedtime. In my oldest son's home, bedtime occurs at the same time every evening. And, almost every evening there is wailing, weeping, and cries of, "But, I'm not tired!" Within just a few minutes of laying down, four boys fall fast asleep most nights. Rest is forced because it's best for these little ones; sheep. And it provides their parents, the shepherds, with a few hours of peace and quiet.

When we don't rest well it affects mood and behavior. A whole range of coping skills and cognitive abilities are negatively impacted. Sleep deprived people tend to not look their best either when running on empty all the time. Tired baggy eyes tell a sleep deprived story. Long term sleep deprivation tends to lead towards ill health too.[72] [73] Getting good quality rest is one of the best things you can do for yourself. And, sitting in front of the blue screen hours a day does not aid in rest. EEG studies, which detect electrical activity in the brain, found that the higher-functioning levels of the brain,[74] like the neocortex we use for analysis and reasoning, go offline when we zombie out in front of media, smart phones, and computers.[75]

When my father put his faith in Christ at the age of forty-four, it marked a monumental shift in our relationship. Having the pleasure to share Christ with him, his life changed remarkably for the better. He became a new creation in Christ. (2 Corinthians 5:17) Dad wanted to grow in his faith. So, every morning at 4:00 am, he began waking to study Scripture, read, meditate, and pray. His rising so early turned him into a grumpy snapping old grouch. No one wanted to be near him. After a few conversations, Dad realized his need to get a little more than five hours sleep a night. Bible reading, and prayer were important, but meant very little in a sleep deprived mind.

Find a special place. Have you ever laid down looking up at the sky in a green pasture? As the wind blows, the clouds pass, and the high grass covers the horizon, rest is found. The sheep, led by their shepherd, lays down in deep grass away from it all in a quiet place. When is the last time you sat by a quiet stream or in a quiet place? Challenging to do in our busy world today, isn't it? There's something special in still waters and green pastures. Explore. Find your quiet place. Schedule times for your quite place to lay down in your green pastures. Make sure your quiet place is a quiet place rather than just another to do list of busyness.

During one of my pastorates, rest and stress were great struggles to find. Living in a very rural area near the Canadian border, I took up photography at the urging of my oldest son. Armed with a used Canon Rebel EOS Camera and set of decent lenses, almost every day off found me in the wilderness exploring nature photography. This became my resting place. My love for photography transformed me into a decent photographer, but most of all it provided mental decoupling and destressing. Traveling often again, stress again presents challenges. My son recently presented me with a couple of new lenses for my old Rebel. It was a hint, "Dad, pick up your camera again. You need it." And, my Facebook recently showed the best four nature photos out of over 150 shots in just one day. Exhale. Thank you, son.

Restore Your Soul Back to Health. Restored *"Shuwb"* reminds us of the purpose of the shepherd, to restore soul-health. Our souls do not live in perpetual health and strength. Sheep under constant dangers from the perils of nature's enemies need stilling, quieting, and rest. Again, understanding the verb stem here is helpful. *"Shuwb"* here is in the Polel stem indicating to "lead away enticingly" to a repairing refreshed place.[76] This wonderful word is also in the Imperfect verb tense indicating "restoreth" an ongoing process of health and frequent repetition.[77] Spend time often with the Shepherd in your green pastures and beside your still waters.

4rd Confidence in the Shephard

Sheep don't know the end of their journey. Following the Shepherd, they take it one step at a time. We try to plan our lives, but much of the journey is unknowable until one arrives. *"We can make our plans, but the Lord determines our steps."* (Proverbs 16:9) Whatever one's level of planning might be, life follows twists and turns of the river bed. Confidence in the Shepherd acknowledges that our lives are not our own, and the soul's existence is of high purpose.

David's confidence in his shepherd focused on the Shepherd's purpose for his sheep rather than the sheep's' desire for themselves. The Shepherd renews and guides a soul, bringing honor to the shepherd's name. (Psalms 23:3) The flock belongs to the shepherd, and ultimately, he knows where to lead his sheep. David, arguably the most powerful man in the world of this time, saw both the beauty of the universe (Psalms 8:3), and the security of a shepherd. *"How precious is your unfailing love, O God! All humanity finds shelter in the shadow of your wings."* (Psalms 36:7).

Soul Living

Healthy souls are prepared to navigate life's trials. *"Even when I walk through the darkest valley . . ."* (Psalm 23:4a). The darkest valley. What is the darkest valley you're facing? For me, my darkest valley led to a diagnosis of PTSD a few years ago. Years of helping AIDS orphan children in South Africa, took its toll. Keeping personal, emotional distance from the sick little one's proved impossible. The death of a little Zulu girl, Andiswa, set my brain into a jumbled mess trying to cope with incredible vivid imagines of suffering, brutality, and loss. My valley was deep, dark, and terrifying.

The Shepherd does not promise life free from danger. The Shepherd promises to lead his sheep through life's
Valley of the Shadow of Death.

"I will not be afraid, for you are close beside me." (Psalms 23:4b) God surrounded me with several shepherds. Randy, a pastor friend, and his church valued my soul's health. Brenda, Director of Care Ministries, got me in touch with Tom, a Christian Therapist. Through the generous donations of members, all expenses were covered.

Tom taught me how to manage the vivid images of brutality witnessed over the many years of serving in South Africa. In my valley, God – Randy, Brenda, and my sweet wife were close beside me. I learned not to fear what my brain struggled to comprehend. *"Your rod and your staff protect and comfort me,"* became my mantra. Through the pain and struggle of reliving some awful stuff, comfort came, and healing began. In the presence of my enemies, God anointed my head with healing. Once again, my cup, life, began to overflow with blessings. (Psalm 23:5) I learned,

God often brings many shepherds alongside us to help guide us through our Valley of the Shadow of Death. We need to see God's shepherds around us.

"You prepare a feast for me in the presence of my enemies." Enemies seek to rend sheep to bits. David experienced many enemies: The Philistines, Hittites, Moabites, Zobahites, Ammonites, Amalekites, and Edomites made up a list of nations oppose to David. Other enemies sought his demise as well. Depression, sexual wanderings, bad decisions, pride, family strife, and traumatic losses afflicted David throughout his life. David experienced life at the table with his enemies.

"Surely your goodness and unfailing love will pursue me all the days of my life . . ." I learned again, I can count on my Shepherd, and the herdsmen he sends to help guide me through troubled valleys. Souls that seek and follow their shepherd, can live in health and confidence even in dark valleys of struggle. They're able to claim with confidence, *"Trust in the LORD with all your heart; do not depend on your own understanding. Seek his will in all you do, and he will show you which path to take."* (Proverbs 3:5-6)

Ponderings

1. Describe your soul's condition?

2. Who or what currently leads you?

3. What are your thoughts about 23rd Psalm?

4. How might you step closer in relationship with the Shepherd?

5. "The Lord is my Shepherd. I shall not want . . ." What do you want?

6. How does your shepherd take pleasure in you?

-12-
Soul-Consoles
Gratitude and Contentment Strengthening

"Little by little, one travels far."
J.R.R. Tolkien

"It is great wealth to a soul to live frugally with a contented mind."
Lucretius

"Gratitude is the fairest blossom which springs from the soul."
Henry Ward Beecher

In May of 2012, my stepfather, Harry died. It was traumatic as in his last few hours he experienced severe suffering. Repeated calls to hospice in that North Minneapolis hospital failed to bring a response for help until seven hours after our first call. Paper work and arrangements were all in order, but phone calls went unanswered. Unable to prescribe stronger opiates, we stood by watching Harry suffer extraordinary pain. With Harry writhing in pain in the background, voice mails were left for hospice. Shortly after his last breath, hospice arrived, a day late and a dollar short. We were incensed and emotionally wrung out. After he died, we informed our frail ailing mother. Her husband of thirty years just died. Mom asked me to conduct his funeral.

Three weeks later, after a Herculean battle with COPD mom died too. This was slightly unexpected as all assumed she possessed more time. The email came to me during our trip to Thailand. The purpose of the trip was to encourage churches in Thailand, and get away from it all for a while. As we sat by the pool of our hosts, we received the call that mom died. Hastily we cut short the trip after only a few days, and returned to the States. Arriving at the funeral home directly from the airport delirious from jet lag, arrangements for mom's funeral were finalized. Once again, at mom's request, I conducted the funeral. After the grave side ceremony at Fort Snelling in Minneapolis, we retreated to our then home in Northern Minnesota several hours away.

Sitting down exhausted, fatigued, and grieving, I focused on a matching set of end tables in our living room. Cleaning out mom's apartment after the funeral, the end tables were a point of discussion among our siblings. The tables were old, about 1930's, but inexpensive. They were cheap imitations of something grander during that era. Those end tables were not particularly attractive. Not in good shape either as the bottom casters were missing. The consensus was to give the end tables to the Goodwill or Salvation Army. At the last moment, I decided to take them. The tables called out to me. For some reason, I wanted those two old beat up consoles.

During some of my deepest moments of grief losing both Harry and mom within three weeks of each other, I can't explain just how much comfort those two old clumsy pieces brought me. Sitting in my recliner hurting and grieving, I looked at those end tables repeatedly over the next months. The immense comfort they provided intrigued me. I asked myself, "What is it about these tables that bring such comfort? Why is it when I set my coffee cup on one of these end tables, I am comforted. Or, is there something else at work here?" Remember thinking, "This is magical." Was it magical? Was it an allusion? Was it a distraction? What was it about those two end tables that provided so much comfort during my following months of mourning?

I concluded that the tables in themselves meant very little. What those end tables provided was a means of refocusing my soul from hurting losses upon better memories of life with Harry and mom. **If my soul focused on me, my hurts, my feelings, and my thoughts, I hurt.** Deep down inside the recesses of my being, pain resided. Upon looking at mom and Harry's end tables, my soul refocused. My thoughts moved away from self-concentration and hurt. To something better. To something deeper. When I thought of the Twinkies, jelly beans, spearmint leaves, and other junk food Harry loaded on top of those consoles sitting in front of the TV, I smiled. Every time I opened the drawer, my mind went back to mom, who crammed unbelievable amounts of junk in those end tables. I smiled.

Sitting between those two coffee tables over the next few months brought an inexplicable immense amount of comfort during a personal grievous time. They provided soul redirection. Redirection offered comfort. Comfort offered an opportunity for reflection. I discovered:

A Soul focused solely on itself goes no further than itself.
A soul focusing on better and brighter finds comfort and purpose.

The Bible gives examples of soul consoles. The book of Psalms in the Old Testament is loaded with examples of people during times of struggle looking to something better for hope and security. I like to call these the **Consoles of The Soul**. These spiritual end tables sit in my mind on both sides of my soul. Looking to them quite often offers comfort and encouragement during times of doubt, grief, and pain.

Console of Gratitude

Every Thanksgiving marked a hallowed occasion during my childhood. Thanksgiving always occurred at Grandpa and Grandma's house. Mom's parents were the mark of a traditional American family. As the oldest of all the grandchildren, memories rang from a small family of few, to in later years a gathering outgrowing our grandparents home.

Thanksgiving juxtaposed our family's situation at home. As alcohol consumption increased, dad spent less and less time with mom and eventually us. The fighting, screaming, and yelling subsided only when dad and mom were apart. Then there was that morning. Upon waking and coming down stairs, mom sat smoking a cigarette struggling to puff with a bruised swollen face. A few words revealed her two front teeth missing too. Growing up was like that. Dad finally left.

Thanksgiving at grandpa and grandma's house always provided a reprieve from such familial assaults. Sitting next to grandpa offered the safety of a big strong man foreign to me at home. Those Thanksgivings marked strong consoles of my soul. At grandpa and grandma's house we laughed. We sang. Auntie Sandy played the piano and yodeled. Yes, I did say yodeled. Guess we were a little country way up there in Minneapolis. Singing went on for hours sometimes.

The centerpiece of that Thanksgiving experience was the carving of the Turkey. Grandpa always pulled out the electric knives. As we all sat around the table, one by one everyone each recited one thing for which they were thankful. Remember once, my little brother Bob, wasn't even four years old at the time. He burst out, "White cake, white cake, white cake! All we get around here is white cake! I'm "thankful for chocolate cake," as his eyes focused intently on the chocolate cake on the table. Everyone howled in laughter. In that one moment of Bob's thankfulness for black cake, there was no home traumas, no swearing, no drugs, no alcohol, no assault; none of that. For that one solitary moment, I was free. As soon as the laughter died down a cousin piped up, "I'm thankful for chocolate cake too!" Laughter ensued again. During those multitudes of thanksgivings, a beautiful piece of turkey was always placed on my plate smothered in grandma's perfect gravy.

Gratitude Diverts

A wonderful truth occurred during those adolescent years. A truth, which through many turbulent years while growing up, secured this soul repeatedly; a soul-console. In one moment of gratitude was escape. In that moment, gratitude brought balance. In those few minutes, gratitude healed. When gratitude diminished, comfort weakened.

Gratitude Redirects

Gratitude helps move us from anger, pain, and injury. Sure, injury is a reality, but gratitude encourages attention towards the good surrounding us rather than hurt that assaults us. Gratitude deflects feelings of misfortune. In gratitude, respite from my trouble and suffering at home brought me comfort. Suffering already caused pain. Why focus upon the pain thereby adding only more ache to that which already hurts? Gratitude fends off hosts of assaults on one's soul. Thankfulness becomes a powerful shield against soul debilitation. To this day, mastering the art of gratitude continually redirects from that which is tainted towards that which is good and better.

Gratitude Benefits

Robert A. Emmons, Ph.D. specializes about gratitude. He is a professor of psychology at the University of California, and the founding editor-in-chief of The Journal of Positive Psychology. He espouses the physical, social, and mental health benefits of gratitude. In his article, *Why Gratitude is Good,* he answers a question, "What good is gratitude?" He lists several benefits:

1. Gratitude allows us to celebrate the present magnifying positive emotions.
2. Gratitude blocks negative toxic emotions.
3. Grateful people are more stress resistant.
4. Grateful people have a higher sense of self-worth.[78]

As Emmons focuses on gratitude's psychological health of an individual, people long ago discovered its many benefits. Gratitude was not just an end. It was more a reflection one's soul-health.

Gratitude Reflects

Old Testament people didn't use gratitude as a tool simply to achieve purpose and fulfillment. For them, gratitude directed one's thanksgiving towards God. King David sang, *"Bless the Lord, O my soul, and forget **none** of his benefits."* Psalm 103:2 (NASB) Forget none of his benefits. What benefits? Here, David lists an extensive diagnostic list of good things in his life attributed only to God. The end table of gratitude in the 103rd Psalm reminded David of God's goodness:

1. God pardons sin – vs. 3
2. God heals sicknesses – vs. 3
3. God gives worth – vs. 4
4. God wraps in love – vs. 4
5. God fills life with good stuff – vs. 5
6. God gives purpose – vs. 5
7. God makes everything purposeful – vs. 6
8. God did these things for other people, he can do them for us too. vs. –7
9. God is patient and loving – vs. 8
10. He doesn't stay angry for long – vs. 9
11. God doesn't give people what they deserve when doing wrong – vs. 10
12. God is not harsh – vs. 10
13. God's love is too wonderful to understand – vs. 11
14. God does not throw back in one's face their wrongs. In fact, he forgets them – vs. 12
15. God is a faithful father – vs. 13

16. God truly knows and understands – vs. 14-16

17. God is always there for me – vs. 17

18. God is great! He is in control – vs. 19

19. Even angels follow God's lead – vs. 20

20. God is so awesome, everything looks to him – vs. 22

In all these things David concentrates on gratitude towards a loving giving God. Another song writer in Psalms adds to gratitude's crescendo, *"What can I offer the LORD for all he has done for me?"* (Psalm 116:12) In the USA, where consumerism hits its high-water mark, gratitude is difficult for Americans to grasp.

Gratitude Combats

Sitting here in Starbucks writing these very words, I am reminded of just thirty minutes ago. Standing behind only one other customer, I waited. Five employees stood behind the counter while the woman ordering struggled to order, pay for her order, and collect her order. Then a conversation about a funeral ensued. Waiting, and waiting, I waited. Being from Minnesota, I usually handle such things in a passive aggressive way. So, inside thoughts went through my mind. "Just order lady, will yah! Hey, right here, there is another customer waiting! Wonder if that's the first time this guy ever rung an order up? Now, I remember why I don't come here much. Where's the efficiency people?" No, I didn't just make that up. That's how severely depraved my spirit of ingratitude is sometimes.

Finally, just as my order began, another employee walked by asking, "Are you being helped, sir?" Under my breath, I literally said,

"Sure, ask me now while you stood there for ten minutes looking stupid."
I can be a grumpy bugger underneath it sometimes. Finally, I sat down with my Three-shot Grande Toffee Nut Extra Hot Latte, and an incorrect Danish order. Thought, "You can't even get that right, can yah?" As I bowed my head to say grace, "Dear Lord, thank you for..." I broke into laughter. An arrow of shallow self-righteous selfishness struck its mark. Continuing, I redirected my prayer steering my heart's ship towards gratitude. My attitude changed abruptly. "Thank you Lord for this hot coffee, made from clean, drinkable water, and this contamination free Danish warmed for me laced with cinnamon swirls, sitting in this air-conditioned building, on this padded chair, with my laptop, smart phone, leather bound journal, listening to music on Spotify with my Bose Headphones. Thank you for employees who think enough of work, to arrive this morning, open this store, and prepare my order. Oh, and Lord, please forgive me for being an ungrateful grumbling complaining ingrate. In this I pray, uh-hem, Amen . . .?"

Gratitude Serves

Robert Emmons asserts that we Americans are not very good at gratitude because often when Americans express gratitude it's based solely on their good fortune as they perceive it. I'm glad I've got a good job, pretty wife, good kids, and I'm healthy. I'm thankful.[79] But, authentic gratitude is more an admission of dependence upon something or someone. "Gratitude means admitting that we're not fully independent – which can be a scary thing."[80] In the Bible, gratitude is most often directed towards God. In today's postmodern era of serve me, love me, it belongs to me, is it no wonder Americans struggle with gratitude?

Currently, we are spending the summer with our oldest son and his family. In their old farmhouse of 2400 square feet currently dwell twelve people. Yep, 12! In the mix of children are several foster-children with special needs. Spending the summer with my foster-grandchildren encourages development of what I call the gratitude-serve. In serving these precious suffering children, one learns to put their special needs first. Rather that cultivating a retirement, me-first, let's just be comfortable in old age attitude, servanthood strives for mastery.

Gratitude Admits

A soul, nephesh, focused only upon itself dwells mostly within itself. David understood this. He sings, *"How long shall I take counsel in my soul, Having sorrow in my heart all the day?"* (Psalms 13:2 NASB) Considering the heavenlies through Hubble's or Kepler's telescopes produce both a sense of awe and gratitude. Awe at the magnificence of what's out there. Gratitude and admission that I am dependent upon something bigger than me. I depend upon the Sun's heat and light for survival. The elliptical orbits of our solar systems provide order and life.

Watching a mother embrace and kiss a young child pricks gratitude. Motherhood lives for other than itself. A father playing ball with his son, stirs gratitude in that there are some dads who get it. Adults taking time to visit their aging parents shows love and respect above self.

Gratitude admits that I am dependent on something and someone. Ordering that meal at the restaurant depends on the server taking the order and the Preparer cooking the meal. That one meal is dependent on a store owner or corporation fiscally providing for the mere existence of that establishment. My recent trip to the clinic reminds that health care is dependent on a whole group of medical professionals making it possible to see a nurse or doctor. Driving my car to this coffee shop is dependent upon road maintenance, good streets, working traffic lights, and courteous drivers making room for my vehicle. Everyone is dependent. No one is independent. We are all wards of each other.

Console of Contentment

"A man might have a hundred children and live to be very old. But it he finds no satisfaction in life . . . it would have been better for him to be born dead." (Ecclesiastes 6:3) Sobering words. Solomon, "The wisest man who ever lived," ruled Israel after his father David. A unique mark of Solomon's life was his journey to experience all, and write about it. Solomon sought to experience life. All of it. Money, power, position, wealth, career, ambition, worship, sex, and polygamy. He experienced all. Among his greatest feats and accomplishments was his search for true wisdom. It was said of him, *"Solomon's wisdom surpassed the wisdom of all the sons of the east and all the wisdom of Egypt. For he was wiser than all men . . ."* (I Kings 4:30-31)

Contentment is Wealth

This guy who possessed everything boiled life down to contentment. Surrounded by wives, mistresses, wealth, servants, and power he discovered, *"He might live a thousand years twice over but still not find contentment. And since he must die like everyone else — well, that's the use?"* (Ecclesiastes 6:6) What's the use?

Now, just for a moment, let's consider how much wealth Solomon possessed. Looking at only his gold assets, it's recorded that in just one year, he received twenty-five tons of gold. This wealth came in taxes from world travelers and merchants. One ton of gold today equals a little over 28,000 troy ounces today. Times that number by 25 tons, and Solomon received over 700,000 troy ounces of gold in one year's period. At a gold price of $1300.00 hundred dollars per troy ounce, it totals nearly $910,000,000. It's recorded that Solomon collected this sum consequently every year.

Some doubt Solomon, an ancient king among a primitive people collected such large sums. Evidence exists that some ancient leaders collected more. In societies where private ownership was limited, and monarchies exacted much from their people, it's not unreasonable that Solomon did indeed build a vast financial empire. "Kenneth Kitchen, *The Reliability of the Old Testament* [133-4], notes similar and larger amounts received and bestowed by kings: A single gift of 150 talents was given by Metten II of Tyre to Egypt; Thutmosis III of Egypt gave over 200 talents to a temple, and Oskoron I gave away 383 tons (not talents) of gold and silver in the first year of his reign, 17 times Solomon's yearly take. That makes Solomon, if anything, a pretty modest receiver."[81][82] Alexander the Great took vast sums of wealth during his military exploits from Persia. After defeating the King of Persia, Darius, at Issus, Alexander raided the treasury of Persia. The young King's wealth surpassed imagination.[83]

"Alexander the Great, supposedly took 40-50,000 talents of gold and silver bullion, plus 9000 talents of coined gold, from the royal Persian treasury, as well as 120-180,000 from surrounding cites."[84]

It's safe to say, that in his day, six hundred years before Alexander the Great and hundreds of years after the great Pharaohs of Egypt, Solomon probably was the richest man alive at that time. He possessed everything by today's standards. He achieved the American Dream. Later as age crept upon him, what does he conclude about life in general? Did he conduct a How to Gain Wealth seminar like so many today? No, he concluded, *"What the eyes see is better than what the **soul desires**. This too is futility and a striving after the wind."* (Ecclesiastes 6:9 NASB). Solomon concluded it better to enjoy that which one possessed right now, right in front of you, then to look for something bigger, better, happier somewhere else.

Epicurus, the founder of Epicureanism six hundred years later wrote much the same, *"Do not spoil what you have by desiring what you have not; remember that what you now have was once among the things you only hoped for."* Here an ancient Greek scientist and philosopher observed what yet still troubles so many twenty-three hundred years later. Desiring what one does not possess. Consumerism, the hunt for more and something better, must have haunted people in many societies before our current modern era.

Failing to enjoy that within our grasp spoils our souls as we seek for more, improved, significant, and something to make us hopefully feel happier and better.

Contentment is Career

Blessed with many acquaintances and friends, Jim is an individual greatly admired. His opinions and perspectives are much sought after. Jim retired from Coca Cola and serves as an executive pastor at a very large and influential church. During many discussions, Jim once mentioned a common ailment that afflicts many professionals in the business world. He called it, "Destination Disease." It occurs with some professionals in good jobs making good money. Just about when they settle into their role and responsibilities, they ponder, "Wonder what's over there? Maybe the destination over there on that other career-hill is better. I'm off to that destination to see what awaits." Every three years or so, they're off to another better place "advancing" their career.

I asked Jim about the wisdom of early retirement from Coca Cola. Still young at the time, there was room for advancement. He might have made it to the top! He looked at me and smiled, "Today, right this moment, serving in my church, I am at the top. I'm content. This is my wealth. I've learned to look no further than that which I enjoy right now."

Discontent Wants More

Consumerism is now part of the very fabric of life in America, and around the world. Since the 1950's, people consumed more than all the total populations living before us.[85]

The struggle with stuff is not with the stuff we currently own, but with the stuff we believe we must yet obtain. The only hope of our economy surviving in its current form is through consumerism;

convincing people they need that which they rarely consider. Repeated presentations of unknown products create a thirst to own the previously unknown. American garages throughout the United States assist in proving this point. Garages throughout America are stuffed to the brim with everything and anything except automobiles. Filled to the ceiling with stuff, most automobiles sit in driveways due to lack of space.

The Dalai Lama's words challenge, *"When you are discontent, you always want more, more, more. Your desire can never be satisfied. But when you practice contentment, you can say to yourself, 'Oh yes - I already have everything that I really need.'"*[86]

My Soul's Consoles

These two Soul-Consoles mark my changed life and attitude. Pastoring in the United Sates and missionary work in South Africa over the past almost 40 years refocused personal attitudes about "my" stuff. Funerals helped change personal values towards stuff. Don't get me wrong. I own stuff. However, I try to hold only that which I need appreciating its value and worth. Beyond stuff there is so much more; family, grandkids, sons, daughters, relationships, and coffee on a cool night in Wisconsin when my five-year-old grandson asks a question after playing with him for the past two hours, "Papa, why are you so silly?"

One point emphasized with every family of every funeral I conduct concerns behavior and words. A warning is usually offered, "Be very careful what you say to each other and how you treat each other during your times of grieving. Many family members after a funeral never speak to each other again because of painful words spoken during a funeral . . ." It's tragically amazing the words family members exchange with each other during a funeral of a family member.

The number one point of friction in most funerals I've conducted is the underlying molten lava of envy between siblings about mom and dad's stuff and money. Just yesterday morning while at a coffee shop, the server behind the counter shared with a customer friend her dismal disappointment with her grandmother's funeral. "We did everything for her. But, they never even visited her. Grandma gave everything to them. I'm not talking to them again. That's for sure." I've literally watched family members come to blows before their dead parent is even in the ground. The fight? Who gets mom and dad's stuff. After that last few funerals conducted, Kathy and I concluded, that at our stage of life, stuff weighed us down. We went on a campaign to give much of our things to family members. We are minimalists at heart now, and we're freer for it.

Gratitude and Contentment are two Soul-Consoles securing my soul. Repeatedly, glancing upon the end tables of contentment and gratitude helps the soul find balance. By learning and seeking to master gratitude and contentment, a soul finds fulfillment.

Ponderings

1. What soul-consoles brings you comfort?

2. For what are you grateful?

3. What contents you?

4. What happens when you focus mostly on yourself?

5. What are your thoughts about:

A Soul focused solely on itself goes no further than itself.
A soul focusing on better and brighter finds comfort and purpose.

-13-
Soul-Anchors
Preventing Drift into Dangerous Waters

"We should not moor a ship with one anchor,
or our life with one hope."
Epictetus

Every summer marked a highlight of boyhood. Anticipation began in May for "vacation" at Great Grandpa and Grandma's cabin. Nestled on a channel connecting two lakes stood a small yellow two bed cabin. My great-grandparents built the little cabin in the 1940's. Great Grandpa died of a stroke in 1959, and it fell upon my grandfather, the only son, to manage the family property.

Earliest memories of that cabin anchored a five-year-old boy in a nuclear family where we all sat at the table together for dinner. Dad, mom, grandpa, grandma, myself, and two siblings crowded around that little table. It was divine. Soon however, dad was out of the picture. After that one summer, the gathering took place without a dad.

Grandpa stepped immediately into my father's role. It was at that lake, "way up North" I learned how to fish for Walleye, Northern Pike, and a host of other creatures teaming under the waters just outside of the front porch of the cabin. Trolling was grandpa's favorite method of fishing. Trolling involved dropping a lure to a certain depth, and dragging it behind the boat. The forward motion of the boat kept the artificial bait active deceiving fish to strike the lure. Grandpa loved trolling. He loved observing wildlife and cabins on the rugged hills of the shore line. We enjoyed it because we caught fish. We enjoyed grandpa.

The Maryanne

The Maryanne, named after great grandma, was a 1950's 18ft wooden hull Chris Craft boat. Grandpa jettisoned the 75 horsepower, preferring a Mercury Hurricane Mark 25 outboard motor. Remember him saying, "With so many family members using this boat, that 75 horsepower would have killed someone!" Summer after summer, grandpa drove that beautiful old lunker up and down the shore lines of Roosevelt Lake dragging our various spinners, lazy Ikes, and spoons from great grandpa's trolling rods. It was magic two weeks of life.

Upon reaching thirteen, as the oldest grandchild, grandpa began in earnest giving boating lessons. We began in his 14 ft. Alumacaft bare bones fishing boat. Grandma bought it for him one Christmas. It affectionately became known as grandpa's boat. In that aluminum bottom boat with a 5-horse power Johnson motor, grandpa taught me the art of captaining. From a thirteen-year-old's perspective, my first time out, felt as if I captained as ship through the Great Lakes. That first time was a proudest and rewarding moment.

In many instructions and trainings grandpa offered On the Job Training. Anchors were almost a lesson in themselves. "You've got to make sure you take the right anchor for the right boat. Never head out into the lake without your anchors. Weather changes, engines stall, and things get rough if the wind picks up. If you've got nothing to slow you down, the wind will blow you into someone's dock or boat. You can get hurt." Looking squarely into my eyes he demanded, "Buddy, you got that?"

In the boathouse, were an assortment of anchors. Small ball and mushroom anchors sat in a corner of that dwelling. In another corner, two heavy scoop anchors laid against the wall. The scoop anchors with broad hooks were heavy and clunky. When cast overboard, the anchors settled on the lake. As the wind pushed the boat, the anchors dug deep stabilizing the boat above. They were perfect for that old heavy wooden haul of the MaryAnne.

The next summer a promotion in personal boating status occurred. It was saddening to hear that the old boat would go to another relative. During its last summer on Roosevelt Lake at the summer cabin, grandpa desired that his oldest grandson enjoy the opportunity to drive the MaryAnne. It marked another proud, confident building moment. After several lessons, grandpa felt confident in his oldest grandson's ability to captain the family boat. That summer was the last time to see the grand old lady on the lake.

Which Anchor?

One morning, a cruise up and down the lake was organized. Intending to spend the day on the lake, the MaryAnne was loaded with coolers of drinks, food, snacks, and fishing gear as we prepared to launch. Entering the boat house, I reached for the scoop anchor. The old steel weight proved heavy and cumbersome. On a bright, clear sunny morning, what might be the actual need for such an old heavy burdensome thing?

Opting for two much smaller mushroom anchors we finished loading and shoved off. Coasting down the South West side of the Lake, we reached Woods Bay. In this Bay, surrounding high hills and trees provided fishing on water still as glass. Fishing most the morning, near noon, the skies began to darken. After an hour, it was clear, the weather grew severe. We headed out of the bay through two small channels into the wide-open waters of the Roosevelt. From the clam waters of the bay to the choppy waves of the lake concerned everyone. The waves began crashing up and over the boat.

A very long lake of over 8 miles, our journey was slow and tedious. Due to the rain, wind, and waves, we managed a bare crawl of speed. Rain fell so hard and furious visibility was nonexistent. The MaryAnne crashed against the waves hurling breakers of water into the boat. We were all scared now. Then it happened. A small sputter, and nothing. That old motor died. As the wind blew us into an indiscernible direction, I kept pushing the electric start button to fire the old motor. Nothing. The wind drove us madding in a direction impossible to discern in the pounding rain. Quickly, we cast both anchors overboard. Problem.

While two small 5-pound Mushroom anchors usually proved adequate for grandpa's boat, they came far short of what The MaryAnne, needed. The winds and waves rocked the boat driving us towards an unseeable shoreline. Then it happened. Crash! The MaryAnne driven by the storm ran aground into a 30-foot dock protruding from the shoreline. We grabbed onto the dock, tied the boat, and rode out the storm. Forty-five minutes later, on a glass calm lake, grandpa approached in his boat.

Managing to start the MaryAnne after several hours we limped the injured old lady back to the cabin. The next morning grandpa asked for a conversation.

"Buddy, remember what I told you about anchors?" Bowing in shame I replied, "Yes, sorry, grandpa." He continued, "I am glad you, your brothers, and sisters are ok. That is the main thing. But, great grandma's boat is pretty banged up. That's your fault. You didn't follow instructions on the anchors. Right?" Acknowledging the discernable error became a lifelong lesson still with me more than forty years later. My error cost grandpa time and money repairing the boat before handing it over to his sister.

Dangerous Anchors

In 1883, in Glasgow, Scotland, the *SS Daphne* was launched into open waters. She sank almost immediately drowning 124 workers on board. The cause of the sinking showed in its anchors. Around 200 workmen were on board as they launched the ship. The workers intended to begin fitting the 450-ton Daphne as soon as she was properly afloat. As per the usual practice, anchors were attached by cables to each side of the ship providing stabilization of the vessel as it slipped into the waters.

As the *Daphne* lurched into the river, the anchors failed to stop the ship's forward progress. The starboard anchor moved only 6-7 yards, but the port anchor was dragged 60 yards. The currents of the river caught the *Daphne* flipping it over onto its port side. She sank in deep water. Around 124 died, some sources say 195, including many young apprentice boys, some of whose relatives watched the ceremony from shore.[87]

"The cause of the disaster was reported to be little initial stability combined with too much loose gear and too many people aboard."[88] Laws changed reducing the number of workers on board to those necessary for mooring and stabilizing a vessel. They raised, repaired, and renamed SS Daphne, the Rose.[89]

As with the *Daphne,* many anchor their souls poorly. Weights thought to secure, fail to prevent a soul's drift towards dangerous rocky ground. Life's shoreline is strewn with the wreckages of poorly anchored souls. Improperly weighted misapplied anchors, trusted for security by owners, present huge hazards when life's storms beat upon a soul's hull.

Today, anchors are used in a variety of ways. From small boats to large ships, anchors still offer stabilization from battering forces pounding against the hulls. Interestingly, even huge oil platforms utilize different type of anchor systems to keep the floating cities in place. Mooring systems rely upon the strength of its anchors on the ocean floor to keep mammoth platforms from swaying. Vertical load and drag anchors are just two types of anchors used in oil platform mooring systems.[90]

Olympus is a huge oil rig structure in the Gulf of Mexico. At 40 stories high and weighing more than 120,000 tons, 192 people live and work on board this floating empire.[91] How does the Olympus stay in place? What keeps it from swaying and running aground? "The tether system moors the platform to the seafloor about 3,100 feet below by thick pipes. While the platform is floating, it doesn't sway. Walking on it feels about as solid as being on land."[92]

Personal observation puts most people, and their situations, into one of three classed mentioned; the MaryAnne, Daphne, or Olympus. The anchoring systems on these three floating entities answer a lot of life's tough situations. How we anchor ourselves add or detracts to life's qualities.

MaryAnne Anchoring

While anchoring often conjures up weighted items dropped overboard tethered to boats, it also refers to the human emotion. **Anchoring** or **Focalism** is a term used in psychology to describe a common cognitive human tendency to rely too heavily, or "anchor," on one trait or piece of information when making decisions.[93] In Anchoring, people tend to make decisions based upon a single conversation, experience, or initial piece of information.

I like to call it MaryAnne Anchoring. MaryAnne Anchoring results when we make current decisions based solely upon past initial experiences. My initial experience with anchors involved a small, lightweight fishing boat. The anchors always provided needed weight and function for that boat. Therefore, those mushroom anchors must be good enough for all boats. My focalism on that day in the MaryAnne luckily did not end in disastrous results.

1st Experience Anchoring. My dad's laptop computer is a great example. Twenty years ago, someone helped my dad buy the then newest laptop on the market. Dad never owned a computer in his life.

Not knowing how to type, he struggled from the beginning. Several years later that laptop just sat on a book shelve. He asked, "Hey Bud, do you think you can sell this for me?" My answer ignited a firestorm. "Well, dad, I can try, but it's five years old and not worth much now." Dad exploded, "What do you mean by that?! I paid over $800.00 dollars for that laptop." Anchoring in his initial experience, he convinced himself that his laptop was still worth at least the initial purchase price. Ten years later, after his death that laptop still sat on a shelve in his office.

People practice anchoring all the time. A bad experience at a church means all churches are the same. All lawyers are . . .? Used car salesmen are all . . .? All men are . . .? All politicians do is . . . You can't trust women because . . . See what I mean?

The first impressions interacting with an employee anchors judgment of what that business is like. One a person shared, "I never go to Walmart!" He went on to explain his disappointment with a purchased item. He declared, "All they sell there is junk."

Limited Information Anchors. While in California, we shared with a group of business owners our ministry of Missionary to Missionary Care.[94] As several of the people present financially supported several missionaries in various countries around the world, they were very interested. Spending several weeks in the area, one gentleman asked to meet. Over coffee, he posed a question, "Don, what's the deal with your car?"

Just starting our new ministry, we were pinching our pennies. The old Buick was a true "Up North" car. The rocker panels under the doors were completely rusted out. I answered, "It's not much to look at, but it gets us around." The businessman's answer was surprising, "Come down to my car dealership. There are a couple of vehicles we want you to look at. Some of us got together. We are going to buy you a new vehicle."

The next morning, Kathy and I looked at several vehicles. It was our choice. Anyone of them were ours. All we needed to do was just say, "That one." Asking for a week to research each vehicle, we choose a Kia Sorento. I'd never owned a Kia before, but after much research with the choices presented to us, we signed papers on the three-year-old vehicle. The next day, we picked up our new ride, gifted to us by some tremendous people who believed in us.

The owner of the dealership mentioned, "It was interesting to watch you in your process." "How's that?" I replied. He continued, "Well, most people tend to just focus on one major thing when purchasing a vehicle. He explained that often the odometer or mileage is the sole anchor point of consideration. He continued, "I've seen people choose a lesser vehicle over another just because the odometer reading was 10,000 miles less." He explained, other people just look at the price. He went on, "If I lower the price $1,000 from the initial price, often that is the only mitigating factor in their purchase. People often buy a lessor car believing the first thing they looked at was either bad, good, or better."

You seem to have several reasons I see for purchasing this vehicle." "Yes," I replied, "It may have a few more miles, but not many. Without the third-row seating, there is more storage. The options and extras on this vehicle surpassed the two other vehicles you offered. And, the GDI 4-cylinder engine was a big point." Being a GM dealer, he was unfamiliar with Kia and enquired, "GDI?" I replied, "Yes, Gasoline Direct Injected." There is more horsepower than other smaller engines and the fuel economy is better too. The tinted glass was another big reason we chose this vehicle." With that he smiled, and with much appreciation we drove our Kia off the lot.

Event Driven Anchors. A group of psychologists explained focalism or anchoring this way, "The durability bias, the tendency to over predict the duration of affective reactions to future events, may be due in part to focalism, whereby people focus too much on the event in question and not enough on the consequences of other future events."[95] People focus on one event, anchoring all future events experienced in their pasts. Anchors tethered to past experiences tend to set our judgements in handling current issues in life. Once an anchor is set, judgements and decisions are made adjusting away from that anchor.[96] Single events tend to drive future experiences. How often do we do this?

An example of my relationship with my father might explain anchoring or focalism a bit. I prefer to call it **MaryAnne Anchoring**, because it gives me such a powerful personal visual of making decisions based on correct information. My father sort of disappeared when I was ten years old. He and mom divorced two years later. Weekend visits a year later ceased, and then at thirteen dad disappeared from my life. It was ten years before I saw him again. It proved an immense struggle over the years to trust any man older than myself. Perceiving that all men twenty-five years older than myself were untrustworthy. Once understanding my focalism through these personal lenses helped me overcome this poor anchoring.

Souls often cast out anchors that secured them in previous experiences. Problem is, when entering new stormy waters outside the bay, those anchors may not hold. As life changes, one's soul-landscape changes too.

SS Daphne Anchors

That Christmas Eve night with Lon, brought memories of SS Daphne for personal application. As Lon lamented his position in life, employment, family, and church, I posed a question, "Lon, what's securing your soul right now?" With this rather odd question, Lon stumbled. His answer showed he based his feelings on an assortment of anchors ill fitted for his life. Like the SS Daphne, his anchors dragged him down rather than offering stability and stillness of soul.

Anchor # 1 Recognition. "I used to play bass in the church, but someone else took my place. I don't get to play anymore." He went on to explain in detail, twenty years of bass playing in "his church." As programs changed with younger people entering the church, Lon's country western style of a 50 plus year old didn't seem adequate any longer. He complained, "They've got a bass player that does their kind of music now." Contemplating, he wrinkled his nose, "Guess I'll never get that chance again. I miss playing bass."

Asking a probing self-discovery question, I responded, "Lon, is there somewhere else in the church you might be able to play? Or, what about the Rescue Mission downtown? There must be other opportunities to play?" His reply revealed much, "Yah, I guess so, but I'd rather be up front." Lon lived for the limelight of the moment, an experience that is always fleeting. No one lives on stage forever. Without recognition, Lon's me-focused anchor dragged listing his soul to port.

Anchor # 2 Self-Worth. Lon sighed, "Guess, I'm just a dinosaur now. Not good for much. No one really wants or needs me." Lon's lens of self-worth was flawed. If he focused upon youth and the ability of others, he doomed himself to a dark world of self-loathing and depression. The truth was that the talent on the church stage far surpassed him. A simple country style bass player was no match for the incredible talent before us that Christmas Eve. What Lon failed to consider were the opportunities at the local rescue mission, soup kitchen, and campus churches that desperately needed and wanted a bass player. Lon wanted to be someone else. Someone he was not. He lived for the limelight and acknowledgement. That anchor dragged him below the waters of possibilities into the muck and mire of improbabilities.

Anchor #3 Nostalgia. "Use to love helping in the church, but I don't agree with what they are doing here now." Lon went on to explain his love for older materials moaning the use of new materials he didn't care for much. I was trained in the Navigators and Evangelism Explosion, but they don't care about all that now. "Besides," he said, "The stuff they are preaching here today is so watered down. There is no meat in it. I want deep teaching, not all this fluffy stuff. It's just not like it used to be." "Used to be" marked a period in Lon's life more than twenty-five years earlier. Nothing was like it used to be. Nothing. Nothing ever is twenty-five years later.

Anchor #4 Resentment. Lon, continued, "You know the pastor and I used to be so close. We'd meet every week for coffee, and talk about church stuff. But now, hey, you've got to be someone around here to even get his attention. He doesn't even return his emails." Again, Lon looked far back to a time when less than two hundred people attend "his church." During that conversation, the church expected over 7,000 people to attended Christmas Eve services. Clearly, his pastor possessed very little margin of time for such visits. His resentment anchor capsized Lon with inaccurate facts and assumptions. Many drown in their self-pity from a warped reality.

Anchor #5 Bitterness. During the conversation, Lon listed many church people of the past. People who no longer attended the church. With each one mentioned, he listed a grievance, an offense committed against him. In each case, he maintained his pure status of an innocent victim pounced upon by wielding church members. "You can really get hurt around here," he maintained. Lon's anger grew noticeably with each name mentioned. As each name came out, he cast another Daphne anchor overboard. Each weight dragged upon his soul. He visibly and emotionally began to shut down.

Anchor #6 Discouragement. During the conversation, Lon's dejected negative fault finding proved the wrestling place of all his thoughts. Lon weighed himself down with a thousand dark reflections. Now as the storms of job loss, failing health, empty nesting, and relationship challenges blew across his bow, he found himself at the mercy of the winds and waves. Clearly, his anchors caused more harm than good swamping his soul in a harbor of discouragement and depression. Lon was unseaworthy. No wonder attempts to set sail met with failure and continued discouragement.

Anchor #7 Busyness. "I just keep myself busy," he exclaimed. Helps me keep my mind off all this stuff. Busyness helped Lon avoid dealing with the cause of his problems; himself. As Lon flittered back and forth between points frivolity and triviality, he blocked out his struggles. As his avalanche of emotions gained momentum, Lon's struggles buried his soul in self-absorption.

Other Dangerous Anchors

Like the 120,000 Olympus Oil Platform, we need ample tethering to sure anchors. If we are to stand on the decks of our souls in serenity and contentment, better anchors need acquiring. Storms will come. Storms always come. Perhaps, you're currently experiencing an incredible storm. Loss a spouse, betrayal, job loss, income depreciation, health decline, a fracture relationship, a chronic addictive habit, or a world view in a nuclear biosphere full of unrest. The waves beat against your soul's haul. Your soul sways in the buffetings. At any moment, the waves may breech your haul. What to do? Make sure of your anchors.

Wish Anchors. Once I asked my mother why she gambled so much. Mom loved the Lotto, pull tabs, slots, casinos and all the rest. She claimed, "I always at least break even." Mom's "I Never Lose" philosophy landed her in an old mobile home up in Northern Minnesota without a penny to their name. The mobile home leaked, smelled horrible, and was riddled with mold. Just entering the dwelling took my breath away. We all tried to help. A younger sibling and her husband provided for them the last ten years of their lives. When pressed as to the reason for her gambling, mom always replied with the same answer. **"It gives me hope."** Mom always believing she'd hit the mother lode someday. Mom lived with an empty unrealized unrealistic expectation of wishes. One more slot, one more Lotto, one more time, and maybe, just maybe, I win that big one. She always lovingly promised, "And when I do, I'll make all my children's lives better!" Mom refused to ever acknowledge her gambling addiction. That anchor dragged her into the waters of despair often.

Loneliness Anchors. Another time, an elderly church member entered my office. Before a word of conversation began, she broke down into tears. After her husband's stroke, life radically changed. Placing her husband into assisted living, she grew lonely. She found companionship at the local casinos dotted along the many lakes of Minnesota. She cried, "I hoped to find a friend down there." In her loneliness, she squandered her husband's entire life savings away in less than three years. After placing a mortgage on her debt free home, she gambled her home away, and faced eviction.

Hope Anchors. "I hoped it might be different, better, but . . . not like this." Careers also place hope on its mantle. A friend once shared, "I'd hoped this job had place for advancement. I sold my house and moved way down here to Texas. Things were moving along nicely, but then they sold the company to an outfit overseas. I lost my job." "Hope"

– that's a big word. Isn't it? I hoped my marriage worked out better. I hoped my kids did this or that. I hope this or that will turn out. A common reply, "I hope so," speaks volumes beyond an initial response.

I like another quote from the Greek philosopher Epictetus. Epictetus was born a slave. He gained his freedom after the death of the Roman Emperor Nero. As Greek Speaking Stoic Philosopher, he was banished from Rome when Emperor Domitian cast all philosophers out of the city. He traveled to Nilopolis in Greece, where he founded his own philosophy school.

Epictetus taught philosophy as a way of life and practice rather than theoretical engagement. He maintained the only external events controllable is our response to what happens to us. When it came to putting one's hope in an instance of life, he nailed it.[97] **"Neither should a ship rely on one small anchor, nor should life rest on a single hope."** A single hope. Like my mother, many focus their lives on a single hope. Hope on a career. Hope on position. Hope in a relationship. Hope in happiness of things. Epictetus realized much of life occurs in shifting sands. Things change. Communities change. Politics change. Relationships change. Shifting sands. And, one commonality I've observed among all people is that no culture likes change. Yet, everything changes continually.

Church Anchors. As a missionary and pastor for the past forty years, poorly anchored souls bob up and down in the church pews every Sunday. Troops of people exit the church yearly disillusioned and disappointed. Expectations of what the church should mean to me and do for me poorly anchor many souls.

During the writing of this very chapter, I received an inbox on my Facebook from a young woman who attended the church I pastored. They visited the church shortly after my arrival, and became very active. After six years of belonging to the church, a job transfer moved them several hours away. She sent me this message,

> "We really enjoyed attending _____ church while you pastored. Our first Sunday was your first Sunday. But we never ever seemed to crack the shell of that church clique. I'm sure you know who I'm referring to. Anyways, _____ asked me to come back last weekend to sing at Praise 10 with him again. I was so excited to be back. But the response I got was less than welcoming. And to find out later that the snub was very intentional! That I shouldn't have been allowed to come back and participate in the first place. It just makes me sad to know that we're not welcomed back to what we thought was our home church.

Fortunately, my friend is spiritually mature. She cast off that rusty anchor of rejection. Though painful, she cut loose the anchor or denunciation from her soul, allowing her to sail on. Sadly, no tragically, others in that church were not as fortunate. Many placed high expectations upon acceptance and belonging. Spurned of that faction tethered their souls to ruin. Often, I heard the words, "I'm finished with people like this. I'm finished with church."

Acceptance Anchors. A very high profile, influential woman in the congregation said more than once, "It's tough getting in here. But once you're in you're in." Now, a good many people visited that church seeking "community." After a couple of years, a good many left that church too.

One woman commented, "No matter what I do, it's obvious we will never be accepted here. It's so incredibly disappointing. I think I'm pretty much done with church."

Churches often resemble country clubs. Upon joining the church, paying one's dues (offerings), serving in the organization, an expectation of return for services occurs. Upon not receiving a perspective "amount due" disillusionment and frustration occurs. Vessels sailing through the channels of the church out to open waters never return.

Once a woman and her husband entered my office. Sitting down, I knew I was in for a rough ride. Her complaint, "No one visited me in the hospital during my surgery. Or at home during recovery." Later discovering that she'd entered the hospital for cosmetic surgery, a tummy tuck and breast implants. Not a single person in the church seemed to know about it. Claiming the church community didn't care about her, she left the church with her husband and new prosthetics.

A retired couple moved three hours North of the Twin Cities. Way up in Northern Minnesota they hoped to spend their retired years building friendships enjoying their golden years. After five years they shared, "No matter how hard we try we're not accepted. We've tried to join community service groups and get involved in church. But, it's like we're just tolerated." Soon afterwards they moved back to the Twin Cities to reconnect with friends whom they soon discovered moved on with their lives. Now their once close friends seemed distance too.

Leadership Anchor. Answering my phone, Mack began to describe his disappointment with his church. Serving as an elder for the past ten years in a Mega Church, he expressed, "For all my service, this is the gratitude I get." Mack's Senior Pastoral Leadership Team became elusive and inclusive dealing with their elders. When discussing an important decision, he felt the Senior Pastoral Team bullied elders into compliance. Causing much anxiety, Mack suddenly resigned from the board, the church, and departed, "I'll never do that again." Mack cut his ropes. Set his ship loose. He and his family still drift outside the church harbor. He is distant and impersonal towards anyone from his previous church.

Church-staff Anchor. It's tragically interesting, maybe only to me, how many used-to-be church staff members God brings alongside us. A good many Millennials and Xers share their utter disillusionment with the church. Many complaints centers around the same three issues; burnout, loneliness, and finances.

After ten years working on a large church staff, a pastor in his middle thirties said, I can't be a father or husband working sixty hours a week. One of us needs to be home. Since my wife has benefits and better pay we decided that I'll be a stay at home dad. I'm glad to be out of the church. It was a lonely place anyways.

One common complaint surfacing often is that many staff members find only superficial relationships at church. A staff member shared, "I am an introvert, but even I am surprised by how many staff members are lonely. Church members become acquaintances, not friends. Staff families seldom spend time together. Staff themselves are sometimes at odds with each other, especially in struggling churches."[98]

There is no community. Some of the loneliest people I know work at church. Ester Feng in her blog *Lonely Leaders* bares her soul, "God, would you bring me some friends to fill the void? God, is there something wrong with me? Do I need to adjust my expectations? Is this simply a season? What are you trying to teach me?"[99] Loneliness is an anchor pulling many church staff souls off balance.

Carrie Nieuwhof offers good advice, "Solitude is good. It's healthy and healing. **But isolation is a tool used by the enemy.** When I isolate myself, I lose touch with reality, cut myself off from relationships that give life, and expose myself to risks that would never happen if I'm in authentic community. As much as I decide to be lonely, I will be. But I don't need to be."[100]

A third common complaint is compensation for services. It shocks me to no end that churches hire staff expecting them to cope without health insurance, retirement, and other benefits. With student loans reaching astronomical amounts, the church can't compete in the labor force. One gifted young woman said, "I'd love to be on staff at the church, but I can't afford it." Interesting, Senior Lead Pastors often enjoy comfortable lifestyles while their staff serve in deprivation.

Anchors provide stability in stormy waters, or cause a ship to list. Only a true appropriate anchor properly applied can steady one's soul throughout life's journey. Examine your anchors. Cast unworthy anchors aside. Acquire better anchors. Practice deploying them. Then, set sail with confidence and hopeful expectation!

Ponderings

1. Examine your anchors.

    - Describe your hope anchors?

    - What about your expectation anchors?

    - And, your leadership anchors?

    - What about your staff anchors?

    - And, those acceptance anchors?

2. How do you anchor yourself?

3. What anchors might be better discarded?

4. What SS Daphne Anchors do you rely upon?

5. What new anchors can you deploy to offer greater stability?

-14-
Soul-Security
Anchoring Your Soul

"This hope is a strong and trustworthy anchor for our souls."
Hebrews 6:19

"The whole thing is quite hopeless, so it's no good worrying about tomorrow. It probably won't come."
J.R.R. Tolkien – The Return of the King

"One should . . . be able to see things as hopeless and yet be determined to make them otherwise."
F. Scott Fitzgerald

My mother, unknowingly, stumbled onto a soul-truth. Her words, **"It gives me hope,"** points to a common human experience. People need hope. Hope is the difference between simply surviving and thriving. A young couple marries. They hope to buy a house. A career begins with high expectations. Chemo begins with the hope of a cure. A pill is taken in hope it will reduce anxiety. Families leave neighborhoods relocating hoping for a better life. I like English soldier and historian, Captain B. H. Liddell Hart's words, "Helplessness induces hopelessness." Exposure to various cultures attests that hopeless people are indeed some of the most helpless people.

In Ladysmith, South Africa, one of our care center affiliates is called, "Place of Hope." At this clinic, African mothers bring their ill children looking for alleviation of sickness assaulting their children. Place of Hope offers beacons of something better. It champions the African spirit and soul. Retired South African Anglican Bishop and Human Rights Activist Desmond Tutu states it well, "Hope is being able to see that there is light despite all the darkness."

Hope is what people look for and need to navigate this life and the next. The question becomes, "To what anchor does a person tether one's hope?" Prodigious types of anchors offer promises of hope. Consideration; **In the tougher storms of life, will they stay your soul's course?**

The Bible encourages us to place our hope in a single place. Putting out to life's sea unprepared causes unforeseen disastrous consequences.

Luke calls the anchor, "This Hope." Hebrews assures, "This hope we have as an **anchor of the soul . . .**" (Hebrews 6:19 NASB) Imagine, an anchor of the soul. The strength of this anchor is qualified as an anchor that's "both sure and steadfast."

Anchors Away

God's Purpose – You are meant for better things

"We are confident that you are meant for 'better things' . . ." (Hebrews 6:9) God's aim for our lives, is better things. My mother's words, "It gives hope," echo here. "Better things," is a major Hope-Anchor. "Better things" undefined might prove rather nefarious if a soul didn't' understand its origin. Hebrews simply explains these "better things" in one phrase.

"Our great desire is that you will keep on <u>loving</u> others as long as life lasts in order that what you hope for will come true." "Loving" here is from the Greek word "spoude" is most often translated "diligence." Luke encouraged these people to continue in diligence to care and love other believers.

God's "better things" is forged in love. Love in our culture seems elusive to define adequately. One loves a spouse, house, job, location, children, flavor of ice cream, and so on. The Bible repeatedly defines love by a single action; **Give.**

"God loved the world so much that he **gave** . . ." (John 3:16a) Love always precipitates self-sacrificing action on behalf and benefit of another. Here, God gives "his one and only Son." Paul echoes this in his letter to the Romans, "But God showed his great love for us by sending Christ to die for us." (Romans 5:8) Again, John – The Beloved, the golden disciple of Jesus, reiterates, "God showed how much he loved us by sending his one and only Son into the world so that we might have eternal life through him." (1 John 4:9) John calls us to purpose by God's example, "We love each other because he loved us first."

Love is exactly what's missing in this old world today. Headlines with News Media prove this statement so very true. What might happen if the world leaders came together in true self-sacrificing love for one another? What would the church look like today if love truly reigned in the hearts of its members? Every church battle I've ever witnessed boiled down to lack of love by usually multiple parties. "Better things" entail living God's purpose out in our lives. This anchors the soul. In God's love for us. In our love for others.

A group of churchy, Bible scholars, tried to trick Jesus one time. They asked him, *"So, hey, ah, Rabbi, teacher, -- Knowledgeable one, 'What is the greatest commandment in the Bible? What's important here?'"* These guys wanted to split hairs over theology. Splitting hairs rarely does anyone any good. Jesus looked them straight in the eye. He told them the answer they already knew deep in their hearts.

"You must love the LORD your God with all your heart, and all your soul, and all your mind. This is the first and greatest commandment." (Matthew 22:37-38) Jesus could have added, "And, you religious know-it-all's already know this. Don't you?" Repeatedly, Scripture teaches that anything apart from self-sacrificing love is void of true lasting significance. Paul in his letter to the church in Corinth, Greece reminded, *"Even if I gave everything I own to poor people including my body but didn't love others, it means nothing."* (1 Corinthians 13:3 My Paraphrase)

God's intends our souls to anchor themselves in his "better things" for us. Our soul's anchor is love expressed to God first and then to others. A soul focused only on self has nowhere else to go but to itself.

God's Promise – You were meant to live in confidence

Here's one of the best verses in all the Bible. *"And this same God who takes care of me will supply all your needs from his glorious riches, which have been given to us in Christ Jesus."* (Philippians 4:19). One can live in confidence knowing God promises to provide for our needs.

Notice, the promise is to provide for our needs, not wants. Not everything we think essential is a necessity of life.

Another favorite, *"Take delight in the LORD, and he will give you your heart's desires."* (Psalms 37:4) This promise proves particularly true during this juncture of life. My current experiences fill the desires of this heart beyond any personal networking abilities or income.

God's Person – You were meant to live in relationship

"And we know that God causes everything to work together for the good of those who love God and are called according to his purpose for them." (Romans 8:28) Hope in God's person gives confidence of relationship with him. This is the "hope" in Hebrews 6:19 (NIV):

"We have this hope as an anchor for the soul, firm and secure."

What at this moment do you hope in? Think about it, if you will. Please put this book down. Spend time contemplating the source of your hope. For many people asked this question, comes the answer, "Well, I really don't know." We can know with certainty the surety of our anchor.

I have written this to you who believe in the name of the Son of God, so that you may know you have eternal life. And we are confident that he hears us whenever we ask for anything that pleases him. And since we know he hears us when we make our requests, we also know that he will give us what we ask for. (1 John 5:13-14).

Ponderings

1. What are your **Anchors**?

2. How do these anchors affect your ability to live a happy contented fulfilled life?

3. How do you anchor your soul?

4. What is your hope for something better?

5. Consider what might bring greater fulfillment in your life?

-15-
Son Risings

". . . like a lamp shining in a dark place – until the Day dawns, and Christ the Morning Star shines in your hearts."

2 Peter 1:19

That morning those many years ago behind my home in South Africa, thickening smoke blackened out the day. Retiring that evening, burning eyes, sore throats, and the smell of burning grass accompanied us to our beds. In the very early hours of the morning, a rumble in the distance approached. Ominous clouds appeared. With flashes of light and crashes of thunder, a place secured on the porch witnessed nature's powerful display. Blowing winds and pounding rain, the storm proved considerably damaging to the Zulu villages outside of Ladysmith. Grass thatch roofs and corrugated iron did not tolerate well the driving rains and straight-line winds. But, in its volatile abruptness that storm proved a great friend. The trauma from that ferocious storm cleared the skies and eliminated the smoky haze.

Above the horizon, The Morning Star arose in the East just before Sunrise. Venus appeared in a crystal, clear cool crisp sky. It was the first time in days to see stars unimpeded by smoke. Now the air stood pure and pristine.

That evening's volatile tempest drove impurities from the air. It was hard to imagine those two days back to back. One-day dark and bleak, and the next soothing, restful, and relaxing.

Amid traumatized laden souls, storms rage. Emotion's winds blow. The tempests can point one towards true North. Sometimes in the gales of life clearing occurs. Above the storms of life, the sun always rises. It's always there. Even in darkness.

The faithful sun never fails to appear. Limited by the senses, emotions cry, "The sun abandons." Yet, regardless of feeling, perspective, or persuasion, this life-giving body faithfully accompanies **all** through **every** experience of life. One is never adrift in life's waters alone. Never.

This soul wandering in the emotions of extreme trauma questioned, "Why am I alone in all of this." The answer came during the storms, "You are not alone my friend. Everything you suffered I suffered before you. I suffer with you now. I will suffer with you in future.[101]"

The Son always rises. The Son adds beauty to life's landscapes. Behind trauma's clouds, the Son appears. Behind a grievous lost, the Son is there. Behind thick hazes of disappointment, the Son still shines. When surrounded by life's murkiness look towards the Son. Christ the Morning Star is ever present announcing a brighter day filled with purpose. The Son arises. Awake! Look towards the Morning Star. The freshness of the morning air awaits you.

"His purpose was for the nations to seek after God and perhaps feel their way toward him and find him--though he is not far from any one of us."

Acts 17:27

About the Author

Don Mingo is the founder of Missionary to Missionary Care and Mingo Coaching Group. He offers a skilled listening ear to compassion workers serving in dozens of countries. He and his spouse, Kathy, travel around the world, offering Life Coaching, Trauma, and Grief Care. As a PTSD survivor, Don believes that in the harsh realities of life is where God touched his soul directing him towards greater purpose. A purpose that only trauma and struggle produced. More about Don and Kathy is available at:

www.M2MCare.org

www.donaldmingo.com

Facebook: M2MCare

Twitter: M2MCare

Instagram: M2MCare

Other books by Don Mingo

Boundaries – 5 Steps to Getting Your Life Back. Helping people overcome addictions with God's help. At Faithway Publishers, Available on Amazon in paperback and Kindle.

Life Boundaries – Balancing Career, Marriage, Relationships, and the Important Stuff of Life. Available on Amazon in paperback and Kindle.

Get Your Life Back! Journal for addiction recovery. Available on Amazon and in paperback

Endnotes

[1] 3 John 1:2 (ESV) All Bible Verses are from the New Living Bible unless otherwise noted.

[2] Cf. Council Of Florence: DS 1314: vitae spiritualis ianua.

[3] http://www.catholic.com/quickquestions/what-exactly-is-a-soul

[4] Lehman Strauss, https://bible.org/seriespage/2-man-trinity-spirit-soul-body

[5] Ibid.

[6] Wimpy's is my favorite breakfast place in South Africa found throughout the country.

[7] https://www.ccel.org/ccel/wesley/journal.vi.ii.vii.html

[8] https://en.wikipedia.org/wiki/Nihilism

[9] Heraclitus quoted in Hippocrates, On The Universe, aph 105.

[10] https://en.wikipedia.org/wiki/Democritus

[11] http://www.gotquestions.org/human-soul.html

[12] http://www.aish.com/jl/sp/bas/48942091.html

[13] Ibid.

[14] https://goddidntsaythat.com/tag/nephesh/

[15] Joel M. Hoffman, https://goddidntsaythat.com/tag/nephesh/

[16] https://en.wikipedia.org/wiki/Nephesh

[17] http://www.huffingtonpost.com/robert-piper/americans-happiness_b_3922148.html

[18] http://www.huffingtonpost.com/2013/06/01/happiness-index-only-1-in_n_3354524.html

[19] https://www.blueletterbible.org/lang/Lexicon/Lexicon.cfm?strongs=H7665&t=KJV

[20] "Statistics in the Ministry." Pastoral Care Inc. Accessed September 2, 2016. http://www.pastoralcareinc.com/statistics/.

[21] https://www.blueletterbible.org/lang/Lexicon/Lexicon.cfm?strongs=H6937&t=KJV

[22] http://www.biblestudytools.com/commentaries/robertsons-word-pictures/mark/mark-8-32.html

[23] Steve. "Helpful-Trumpet-Guide." Helpful-Trumpet-Guide. Accessed September 2, 2016. http://www.helpful-trumpet-guide.com/.

[24] Estrella, Espie. "Types of Trumpets." About. Accessed September 2, 2016. http://musiced.about.com/od/lessonsandtips/a/trumpettypes.htm.

[25] http://nehemiahproject.org/losing-your-soul/

[26] Ibid.

[27] Ibid.

[28] http://www.patheos.com/blogs/peterenns/2015/06/jesuss-crucifixion-not-exactly-a-selling-point-in-the-ancient-world/

[29] Ibid.

[30] Constable, Thomas. DD. "Commentary on Mark 8:32". "Expository Notes of Dr. Thomas Constable". "//www.studylight.org/commentaries/dcc/mark-8.html". 2012.

[31] http://nehemiahproject.org/losing-your-soul/

[32] Amato, Mary. *Guitar Notes*, (Egmont USA, 2012).

[33] https://en.wikipedia.org/wiki/Door_County,_Wisconsin

[34] http://wisconsinwatch.org/2016/05/human-waste-pollutes-some-wisconsin-drinking-water/

[35] http://www.studylight.org/lexicons/greek/gwview.cgi?n=4756

[36] https://www.blueletterbible.org/lang/Lexicon/Lexicon.cfm?strongs=G4559&t=NASB

[37] http://www.preceptaustin.org/1_peter_21.htm

[38] https://www.google.com/webhp?sourceid=chrome-instant&ion=1&espv=2&ie=UTF-8#q=definition%20of%20malice

[39] http://thelawdictionary.org/malice/

[40] http://www.nij.gov/topics/crime/Pages/delinquency-to-adult-offending.aspx

[41] https://www.blueletterbible.org/lang/Lexicon/Lexicon.cfm?strongs=G567&t=KJV

[42] http://www.studylight.org/desk/interlinear.cgi?ref=59002001

[43] http://www.preceptaustin.org/1_peter_21.htm

[44] Ibid.

[45] Ibid

[46] Ibid.

[47] http://www.preceptaustin.org/1_peter_21.htm

[48] Ibid.

[49] Ibid.

[50] James MacDonald, Bob Kellemen, and Steve Viars , eds. *Christ-Centered Biblical Counseling: Changing Lives with God's Changeless Truth* (Eugene Oregon: Harvest House Publishers 2013), 190.

[51] Ibid., 378.

[52] Ibid., 96

[53] Ibid.

[54] http://peterrollins.net/fundamentalisms-reduction-of-crucifixion-to-a-myth/

[55] http://www.stjosephscatholic.org/

[56] John C. Maxwell, *Intentional Living: Choosing a Life that Matters* (New York, NY: Center Street, 2015), 8-9.

[57] 16 Wildly Successful People Who Overcame Huge Obstacles to Get There, February 13, 2014. Accessed August 25, 2016. http://www.huffingtonpost.com/2013/09/25/successful-people-obstacles_n_3964459.html.

[58] Ibid.

[59] "Http://www.aol.com/article/2015/05/06/van-gogh-s-painting-sells-for-66m-nearly-six-times-its-2003-pr/21180474/." Van Gogh's Painting Sells for $66M, Nearly Six times Its 2003 Price. May 6, 2015. Accessed August 25, 2016. http://www.aol.com/article/2015/05/06/van-gogh-s-painting-sells-for-66m-nearly-six-times-its-2003-pr/21180474/.

[60] "Interview to the Press" in Karachi about the execution of Bhagat Singh (23 March 1931); published in *Young India* (2 April 1931), reprinted in *Collected Works of Mahatma Gandhi Online* Vol. 51. As sited in https://en.wikiquote.org/wiki/Mahatma_Gandhi

[61] https://www.matchbookmag.com/daily/417-top-20-oscar-wilde-quotes

[62] http://dictionary.cambridge.org/us/dictionary/english/continuum

63

http://www.studylight.org/desk/interlinear.cgi?search_form_type=interlinear&q1=Ep
hesians+4%3A32&ot=bhs&nt=wh&s=0&t3=str_nas&ns=0
[64] http://www.preceptaustin.org/ephesians_431-32.htm
[65] http://www.preceptaustin.org/ephesians_431-32.htm
[66] Ibid.
[67] https://blogs.ancientfaith.com/glory2godforallthings/2008/01/30/st-isaac-the-
syrian-and-the-door-of-heaven/
[68] Gesenius' Hebrew-Chaldee Lexicon as sited in
https://www.blueletterbible.org/lang/lexicon/lexicon.cfm?Strongs=H7462&t=KJV
[69] https://sleepfoundation.org/media-center/press-release/lack-sleep-affecting-
americans-finds-the-national-sleep-foundation
[70] http://english.stackexchange.com/questions/14876/use-quotation-marks-or-italics-
for-written-quotes
[71] http://tinybuddha.com/blog/are-you-too-busy-5-signs-of-chronic-stress/
[72] https://www.sri.com/work/projects/specific-changes-brain-associated-sleep-
deprivation
[73] http://www.thinkhealthmag.com/how-rest-and-relaxation-benefits-you/
[74] http://tvsmarter.com/documents/brainwaves.html
[75] http://motherboard.vice.com/read/is-watching-tv-actually-a-good-way-to-rest-
your-brain
[76] http://www.biblestudytools.com/lexicons/hebrew/nas/shuwb.html
[77] https://www.blueletterbible.org/kjv/psa/23/3/p0/t_conc_501003
[78] http://greatergood.berkeley.edu/article/item/why_gratitude_is_good
[79] https://positivepsychlopedia.com/2014/11/25/why-americans-are-bad-at-
gratitude/
[80] Ibid.
[81] http://www.tektonics.org/qt/solwealth.php
[82] Kitchen, K.A. – On the Readability of the Old Testament. Wm. B. Eerdmans
Publishing Co. Grand Rapids, Michigan. Pages 133-134.
[83] http://www.coinsweekly.com/en/Archive/The-coins-of-Alexander-III-the-Great-of-
Macedonia/8?&id=67&type=a
[84] http://www.tektonics.org/qt/solwealth.php
[85] https://www.mtholyoke.edu/~kelle20m/classweb/wp/page2.html
[86] The Dalai Lama, quoted in "Orpah Talks to the Dalai Lama," O, the Oprah Magazine,
oprah.com, Aug. 2001
[87] https://en.wikipedia.org/wiki/SS_Daphne_(1883)
[88] Reed, Edward James (1883). Report On The "Daphne" Disaster. London: Eyre and
Spottiswoode. Retrieved 2009-08-15
[89] https://en.wikipedia.org/wiki/SS_Daphne_(1883)#cite_note-3
[90] http://www.rigzone.com/training/insight.asp?insight_id=358
[91] http://www.npr.org/2014/08/06/335282273/up-close-and-personal-with-a-40-
story-oil-rig-in-the-gulf
[92] Ibid.
[93] https://www.sciencedaily.com/terms/anchoring.htm
[94] www.M2MCare.org

[95] Journal of Personality and Social Psychology © by the American Psychological Association May 2000 Vol. 78, No. 5, 821-836

[96] https://en.wikipedia.org/wiki/Anchoring

[97] https://en.wikipedia.org/wiki/Epictetus

[98] http://thomrainer.com/2015/02/frequent-burdens-church-staff-face/

[99] http://www.christianitytoday.com/gifted-for-leadership/2012/january/lonely-leadership.html

[100] http://careynieuwhof.com/2013/05/hey-leaders-loneliness-is-a-choice/

[101] "This High Priest of ours understands our weaknesses, for he faced all of the same testings we do, yet he did not sin." Hebrews 4:15

Made in the USA
Columbia, SC
04 April 2018